A Guide to Tracing Your Westmeath Ancestors

Dedication

To

My husband Joe
and our children
Patrick, Rosemarie, Theresa and Val

A Guide to
Tracing Your Westmeath Ancestors

Gretta Connell

First Published in
2012

Flyleaf Press
4 Spencer Villas
Glenageary
Co. Dublin, Ireland
www.flyleaf.ie

© 2012 Flyleaf Press

British Library cataloguing in Publications Data available

ISBN 978-1-907990-03-8

Cover Illustration:
Eoin Ryan
www.eoinryanart.com

Layout:
Brian Smith

Contents

Acknowledgements

I wish to express my gratitude for the support, advice and encouragement given to me by many people during the course of my research. This book started out as an assignment for a Diploma in Genealogy/Family History Course at the Adult Education Centre, Univeristy College Dublin. I firstly thank the course tutor, Sean Murphy, MA, for his excellent tuition and encouragement. I also thank Mary Farrell, County Librarian for her support; Gearoid O'Brien, Senior Executive Librarian Athlone Library for giving generously of his expertise and knowledge especially relating to Athlone and its environs; Martin Morris, Archivist for giving generously of his expertise and knowledge; Paula O'Dornan, Senior Executive Librarian; Cailin Gallagher, Executive Librarian and all the staff of Westmeath County Libraries who are my friends and colleagues. Thanks also to the principals and staff of the primary schools in Westmeath; Joe O'Meara, Coláiste Mhuire, Mullingar; Fr. Jimmy Murray, Carmelite Presbytery, Dublin; Sr. Claire, Convent of Mercy, Moate; Sr. Maureen, Convent of Mercy, Rochfortbridge; Mrs. Rosemary Eager, Deputy Principal and Mr. Adrian Oughton, Headmaster, Wilson's Hospital School, Multyfarnham and the staff of Westmeath V.E.C.

Others who deserve thanks include; Mícheál Ó Conláin, Westmeath Archaeological and Historical Society; the late Leo Daly, Mullingar; Rev. Declan Smith, Taughmon; Rev. Peter Rutherford, Castlepollard; Rev. Alister Graham, Mullingar; Rev. Graham Doyle, Athlone; Rev. Stephen Lockington, Mullingar; Ruth Illingworth, T.C., Westmeath Archaeological and Historical Society; Peter Wallace, Westmeath Archaeological and Historical Society; Danny Dunne, Mullingar; Billy Standish, Drumcree; William Smyth, Drumcree; Enda Geoghegan, Mullingar; Paul Hughes, Delvin Historical Society; Helen Kelly, Professional Genealogist, Dublin; the staffs of the following institutions: UCD Library; The National Library of Ireland, especially Tom

Desmond; The National Archives of Ireland; Representative Church Body Library, Dublin; the Valuation Office, Dublin; the Registry of Deeds, Dublin; the Civil Registration Office, Mullingar; Meath County Library; Longford County Library; Roscommon County Library, Offaly County Library, Fr Ignatius Fennessy, Franciscan Library, Dublin and Teresa Finnerty and staff Dun na Sí Heritage Centre Moate, Co. Westmeath.

Thanks also to Dr. Jim Ryan and Brian Smith of Flyleaf Press for their support in bringing this work to a successful conclusion, and to Mr John Feeney for his useful comments and suggestions on the final draft.

A special word of thanks to my husband Joe and our children Patrick, Rosemarie, Theresa and Val for their patience and loving support.

Abbreviations

B	Birth
BL	British Library
BM	Dr. Beryl F.E. Moore, and Michael Kenny, Headstones in St. Mary's Churchyard, Delvin, County Westmeath, 1980.
BP	Burgess Papers
CoI	Church of Ireland
D	Death
DED	District Electoral Division
M	Marriage
GO	Genealogical Office
GRO	General Register Office
HR	Hazel A. Ryan, Athlone Abbey Graveyard, Mullingar, 1987.
IFHF	Irish Family History Foundation
Ir. Anc.	Irish Ancestor
IAL	Irish Army List (King James' Irish Army List)
JAPMDI	Journal of the Association for the Preservation of the Memorials of The Dead in Ireland
JS	Jeremiah Sheehan, Ed. Beneath the Shadow of Uisneach: Ballymore & Boher, (Ballymore), 1996.
MS	Manuscript
MWC1	Mícheál Ó Conláin, A Partial List of some Memorials in Westmeath Churchyards.
MWC2	Mícheál Ó Conláin, Inscriptions in Westmeath Churchyards, part two.
NAI	National Archives of Ireland
NLI	National Library of Ireland
PRONI	Public Records Office Northern Ireland
PW	Peter Wallace, Multyfarnham Parish History, Multyfarnham, 1987.
RIA	Royal Irish Academy
RCBL	Representative Church Body Library
RIC	Royal Irish Constabulary
SLC	Salt Lake City
SOG	Society of Genealogists (London)
TC	Town Council
UCD	University College Dublin
VEC	Vocational Educational Committee
WL	Westmeath Library

The counties and provinces of Ireland

Chapter 1   Introduction

Westmeath, formerly a part of the ancient kingdom of Meath, was constituted as a county in 1542. It is situated in the Province of Leinster and bounded on the west by County Roscommon, on the north by Longford and Cavan, on the east by Meath and on the south by Offaly (see map page 10). Westmeath is often referred to as the 'Lake County' and is a popular venue for anglers. The county is predominantly flat and fertile arable land and it has a strong agricultural tradition with 84 % of its 454,104 acres being used for dairy and beef cattle farming. Around 8 per cent of the county is under turf bog which was at one time the major source of fuel.

In 1841 the population of of Westmeath was 141,300, but twenty years later, the deaths and emigration of the Great Famine had reduced it to 90,879. Emigration continued and it is estimated that 46,938 left between 1851 and 1891. By 1891 the population was 65,109, or almost half of the 1841 population. The 2006 census records the population at 79,346.

Evidence of inhabitation as far back as 2000 B.C. is proven by the discovery of Bronze Age Burials in Crookedwood in 1933. Christianity came to Ireland in the fifth and sixth century and monastic sites founded in Westmeath and its environs in this period can still be seen e.g. at Fore and, just South of the Westmeath boundary, at Clonmacnoise. The population is predominantly Roman Catholic (92.2 per cent in 1861) but several other religious denominations are also represented.

The families of Westmeath are a mix of Gaelic, Norman and others. Historically, the area was ruled by the Southern O'Neills and the seat of the High King was at Uisneach Hill. The major Gaelic familiies in these early times included O'Flanagan, MacAuley, MacGeoghegan, O'Melaghlin and O'Daly.

In 1169 Ireland was invaded by Norman Lords and the Kingdom of Meath, which included Westmeath, was given to Hugh de Lacy. He brought people with him with names such as: Plunkett, Nugent and Dalton. Later, in the mid-1650s the Cromwellian Plantation had a major impact on land ownership as Catholic landowners (including the Norman families) were expelled from their lands and forced to move west of the Shannon. It must be remembered however, that a large portion of the population remained as tenants on large tracts of land.

The lives and activities of the various people of Westmeath have generated a huge variety of records, many of which can be useful to the family historian. It is not possible to cover every detailed source of genealogical information relevant to Westmeath within the scope of this work. However the aim of this book is to describe the most relevant material and archives, and to provide background information which will allow you to find further sources. Most of the major records are common to that of other counties; however, some are unique to the county. This guide will introduce you to all of these records and provide guidance on how to access them (on-line or otherwise) and to use them to your best advantage.

Seal of Athlone, 1663

Chapter 2   Conducting Family Research

There comes a time in life when many of us get the urge to trace our family history; to find out where our ancestors came from and what type of lives they led. This often happens when a loved one passes away, or indeed when a child is born into the family. Whatever the reason, this urge usually comes late in life, when the relatives who would have known most have long since gone. The enthusiastic beginner may therefore have an initial feeling that the past generations have taken all of the information with them to their eternal reward. However, this is not entirely the case as all of our lives leave pieces of evidence from which we can build a picture of lost lives. Accessing this information is the subject of this book. The beginner will also soon discover that they are not alone in their interest, and that many other people are carrying out similar searches and are very willing to share their information.

The first step for the beginner is to prepare to receive and organize family information. When you start to collect data you will find that there is a lot of it! It is essential to create a family tree or pedigree sheet in order to keep track of the information as it grows. Otherwise, your notes will be full of possible connections and potential sources. Unless you organize yourself, you will find yourself lost in potential relations, and unable to remember where you found them. Names and dates for each ancestor in a carefully maintained pedigree sheet will allow you to re-enter a search at ease if a further opportunity for information arises. Blank pedigree sheets can be downloaded from one of the many genealogy software programmes available on the internet, or you can keep all your records within one of the many software programmes available.

You should also work from the known to the unknown, i.e. do not presume any connection you cannot prove. Therefore the best place to start is in your own family or household. Ask your elderly relatives what they know, and record what is said, by whom and the date. Elderly neighbours are also a very useful source if the area of residence is known. People in Ireland in past times seldom moved between areas, and stories about families and individuals survive and may be useful. It is important to listen and record and to verify recollection with fact as oral history can get confused with the passage of time. This is not to undermine the importance of oral history as one person's recollection can put the researcher on a path which otherwise would have remained unknown.

If you are lucky enough to acquire primary data store it in a safe place. This may include photographs, memorial cards or remembrance cards, birth, death and marriage certificates, family correspondence, newspaper clippings or a family bible. Some of this may not make much sense initially but could very well prove useful later on.

It is also advisable to trace one line of descent at a time, starting with yourself and moving back one generation at a time. Trying to search several lines at the same time is a recipe for confusion and lost opportunities.

Before you start using public records, it is useful to understand the administrative divisions used in Ireland, and the types of records which exist. These divisions are explained in chapter 3. A successful search may depend on identifying a family's location, and records differ greatly in regard to how 'home' is specified. For example a US gravestone may read 'Here lies Patrick Kiernan of Westmeath, Ireland' and that may be the only piece of information you have. Equally, the address provided in emigration papers may be given as the nearest town e.g. Mullingar or Athlone, whereas the actual address is located in an adjacent parish. There are many options to assist in identifying specific locations. Griffith's Valuation (see Page 82) provides a snapshot of landholders in the mid 19th century and therefore also of the distribution of names within the county. If you have a name of a spouse, also from Westmeath, you may be able to cross-relate the two names to narrow down the search. Equally, the 1901 census will allow you to do the same search. However, many names are locally common and this will not always work.

Another option, mainly for relatives who have left within the last 100 years, is to ask the Editor of local Westmeath papers (see page 105) to publish a letter stating what information you have and requesting readers to reply. It is useful to bear in mind when beginning your search that the popular name of an ancestor may not be the name on official records. For example, several lines of a family might call their first born son James after a paternal grandfather and then one family might decide to refer to their son by their second name, e.g. Charlie in order to differentiate between the James's. Elderly family members or neighbours may be able to help in this situation.

It is also useful to read some background information on the county in order to have a better understanding of the lives your ancestors lived and how events in history may have affected them. This will help you to understand possible local occupations, and also historical events or practices which may have generated records. Many out of print books on Westmeath history can be found at www.archive.org e.g. The Annals of Westmeath, ancient and modern, James Woods, (1907); and The History of the Diocese of Meath, John Healy (1908). See also page 145 for a list of titles that will help to provide interesting background information on Westmeath history and culture.

Visiting Ireland to conduct your own research is not always possible and you may need to hire a professional to research records which you cannot access on-line or locally. The NLI and NAI webpages list names of Professional Genealogists who will carry out research for a fee. The Association of Professional Genealogists in Ireland (APGI) can be contacted c/o Hon. Secretary, 30 Harlech Crescent, Clonskeagh, Dublin 14, Ireland. Email: info@apgi.ie Website: www.apgi.ie

It is hoped that the information contained in this book will assist you in finding long lost Westmeath roots.

THE

PARLIAMENTARY GAZETTEER

OF

IRELAND,

ADAPTED TO THE NEW POOR-LAW, FRANCHISE, MUNICIPAL AND
ECCLESIASTICAL ARRANGEMENTS, AND COMPILED WITH A SPECIAL REFERENCE
TO THE LINES OF RAILROAD AND CANAL COMMUNICATION,
AS EXISTING IN

1844-45;

ILLUSTRA

A

TOPOGRAPHICAL DICTIONARY

OF

IRELAND,

COMPRISING THE

SEVERAL COUNTIES, CITIES, BOROUGHS, CORPORATE, MARKET, AND POST TOWNS,

PARISHES, AND VILLAGES,

PRESEN

HISTORICAL AND   CENSUS OF IRELAND.

ENGRAVINGS OF THE ARMS OF TH
AND OF THE SEALS   GENERAL ALPHABETICAL INDEX

TO THE

DESCRIBING THE ELECTORAL   TOWNLANDS AND TOWNS, PARISHES, AND BARONIES
BY THE
OF

BY   IRELAND,

SHOWING

THE NUMBER OF THE SHEET OF THE ORDNANCE SURVEY MAPS IN WHICH
THEY APPEAR:

THE AREAS OF THE TOWNLANDS, PARISHES, AND BARONIES;

THE COUNTY, BARONY, PARISH, AND POOR LAW UNION IN WHICH THE TOWNLANDS ARE SITUATED;

AND

PUBLISHED BY S.   THE VOLUME AND PAGE OF THE TOWNLAND CENSUS OF 1851, WHICH CONTAINS
THE POPULATION AND NUMBER OF HOUSES IN 1841 AND 1851,
AND THE POOR LAW VALUATION IN 1851.

Presented to both Houses of Parliament by Command of Her Majesty.

DUBLIN:

PRINTED BY ALEXANDER THOM, 87 & 88, ABBEY-STREET,
FOR HER MAJESTY'S STATIONERY OFFICE.

1861.

Three publications used to establish the
administrative divisions of Ireland

Chapter 3.   Administrative Divisions

An ancestor's address is an essential part of their identity as well as being a very important piece of information on which to undertake research. Many Irish names are associated with specific localities. It can therefore be vital to distinguish between Patrick Geoghegan of Ballymore and the unrelated Patrick Geoghegan of Killare. As in the rest of the country, Westmeath was and is divided into different units or divisions for the purposes of Civil or Church (Ecclesiastical) administrative purposes. Some administrations use the traditional divisions (county, townland and parish) whereas others created divisions specifically for their usage (e.g District Electoral Divions, Poor Law Unions etc). Some churches also created their own ecclesiastical divisions to suit their particular structure. Each of these units is explained in the following pages.

It is important to remember that there are wide variations in placename spelling. During the period when these divisions were established, most of Ireland spoke Gaelic or Irish language. Most placenames were therefore originally in Gaelic, and were anglicized by successive British administrations and by local people as English became the spoken language. However, there was an inconsistency in this process which has created variations in placenames.

Civil Divisions

Townland
The townland is the smallest officially-recognised administrative division and can vary in size from as little as one acre to over a thousand acres. There are approximately 1,360 townlands in Westmeath. They are the basic unit of address for most rural people. The Ordnance Survey Townland Maps for County Westmeath, (1838) are a valuable record of the demarcation of townlands. They can be viewed on line at

http://www.osi.ie/public viewer In order to make best use of your time when searching official records it is important to establish at the outset in which administrative division a townland lies. The 1851 Townland Index described on page 26 is the most useful guide for this purpose. Some townland names will occur more than once within County Westmeath and will be found to be common in other counties also. A pocket of land within a townland may also be known by a minor local name or topographical name which has not been officially recorded.

Civil Parish

The civil parish is the most used land division within records. If you cannot identify the civil parish from which your ancestor came, you will not be able to access most records. There are sixty-three civil parishes in Westmeath each of which contains many townlands. Some Civil Parishes cross county and barony boundaries. The Church of Ireland parishes normally equate to the civil parishes whereas Catholic parishes often vary. - see map and table pages 19 and 20.

Barony

The term barony as a unit of land was introduced by the Anglo-Normans but is generally based on the ancient 'tuath' or territory of an Irish clan. The information in the land surveys of the 17th century was arranged by barony and the barony name continued to be used in some sources recording ownership and distribution of property. It is rarely used otherwise. Westmeath is divided into twelve baronies namely: Brawney, Clonlonan, Corkaree, Delvin, Farbill, Fartullagh, (Demi)Fore Kilkenny West, Moyashel and Magheradernan, Moycashel, Moygoish and Rathconrath. A Barony can straddle county borders as in the case of Demifore. see barony map on page 21.

Poor Law Union

Poor Law Unions (PLU) were introduced under the Poor Law Act of 1838 which was established to deal with the widespread poverty of the period. It was the area within which a tax (or 'rate') was payable by land-holders to maintain the poor. The PLU was based on an area around a large town and most are named after this town. Note that they could incorporate parts of adjoining counties. Each union supported a workhouse within which the neediest cases were housed. for further details. The Poor Law Unions in Westmeath were: Athlone, Ballymahon, Delvin, Granard, Mullingar and Tullamore.

The Civil Parishes of County Westmeath

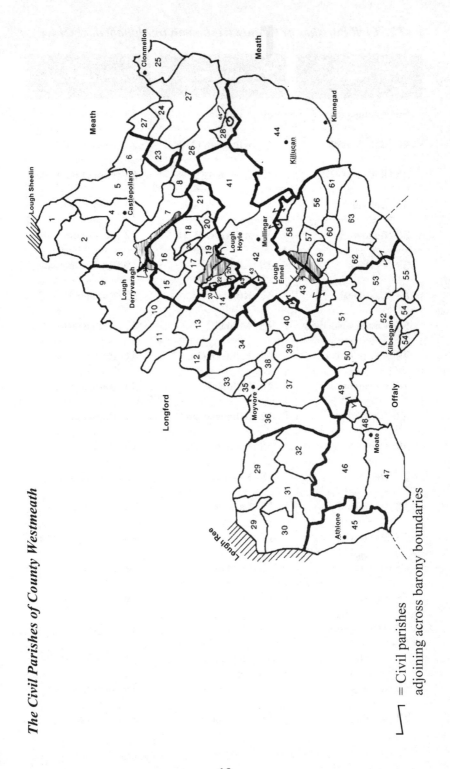

⌐ = Civil parishes
adjoining across barony boundaries

The Civil Parishes of County Westmeath in Alphabetical Order

Map No.	Civil Parish	Map No.	Civil Parish	Map No.	Civil Parish
50	Ardnurcher	60	Kilbride	53	Newtown
46	Ballyloughloe	47	Kilcleagh (2 pts)	29	Noughaval
36	Ballymore	23	Kilcumny	61	Pass of Kilbride
38	Ballymorin	49	Kilcumreragh	33	Piercetown
30	Bunown	31	Kilkenny West	22	Portloman
59	Carrick	28	Killagh	19	Portnashangan
63	Castlelost	37	Killare	55	Rahugh
51	Castletownkindalen	25	Killua	11	Rathaspick
40	Churchtown	44	Killucan (2 pts)	41	Rathconnell
24	Clonarney	26	Killulagh	34	Rathconrath
62	Clonfad	12	Kilmacnevan	4	Rathgarve
39	Conry	48	Kilmanaghan	10	Russagh
27	Delvin	8	Kilpatrick	5	St. Feighins
32	Drumraney	15	Lackan	6	St. Marys
54	Durrow	17	Leny	45	St. Marys, Athlone
43	Dysart	2	Lickbla	18	Stonehall
58	Enniscoffey	56	Lynn	9	Street
7	Faughalstown	3	Mayne	21	Taghmon
1	Foyran	57	Moylisker	14	Templeoran
52	Kilbeggan	42	Mullingar	35	Templepatrick
13	Kilbixy	16	Multyfarnham	20	Tyfarnham

20

The Baronies of County Westmeath

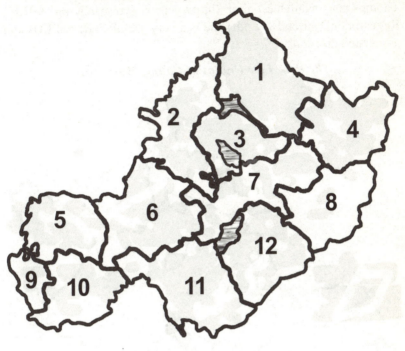

1 *Fore (part in Meath)*
2 *Moygoish*
3 *Corkaree*
4 *Delvin*
5 *Kilkenny West*
6 *Rathconrath*
7 *Moyashel and Maheradermon*
8 *Farbill*
9 *Brawny*
10 *Clonlonan*
11 *Moycashel*
12 *Fartullagh*

These units are also important because the same areas were later used for the civil registration of births, marriages and deaths. For registration purposes, the PLU was redefined as the Superintendent Registrar's District. Under the Local Government Act of 1898, the Poor Law Unions were used for electoral purposes and named District Electoral

Divisions (DEDs). "Registration Districts of Ireland" by Michael J. Thompson is available online (http://genealogyresearch.org.uk/IRL_RegistrationDistricts1871.pdf) and is a very useful guide to PLUs and associated divisions.

The Poor Law Unions of County Westmeath

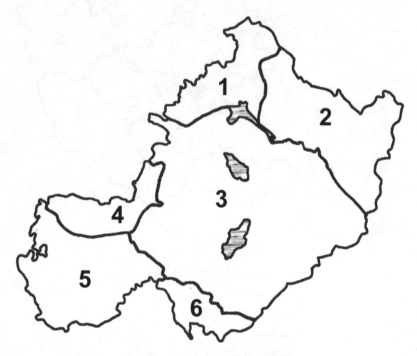

1 Granard (part in Longford)
2 Castletowndelvin (Delvin)
3 Mullingar
4 Ballymahon (part in Longford)
5 Athlone (part in Roscommon)
6 Tullamore (part in Offaly)

District Electoral Division

The District Electoral Division (DED) is a sub-division of the Poor Law union, in which census information was compiled and in which the census returns are also arranged. They were also used for the elections of local and national representatives established under the Local Government Act of 1898.

Ecclesiastical Divisions

The main denominations in Ireland are the Roman Catholic and Church of Ireland (See page 57). Both of these have the same administrative structure of dioceses (under the control of a bishop) and parishes, although there are some boundary differences. Other denominations have widely differing administrative structures which are described in Irish Church Records (Flyleaf Press 2001)

Church of Ireland Parish
The Church of Ireland and civil parish boundaries are normally identical. This is because the Church of Ireland was responsible, until 1858, for a range of civil functions which included Probate (proving of wills) and granting of marriage licences. Church of Ireland administrative areas were therefore de facto part of civil administration at this time.

Catholic Church Parish
Catholic Church parish boundaries rarely conform to those of the Civil Parish, even though they may have the same name as the Civil Parish in the locality. They are often of ancient origin and generally larger in size than Church of Ireland parishes. Catholic parish boundaries were regularly changed to cater for changing populations, and new parishes were created where required. Most of Westmeath lies in the Diocese of Meath with parts in the Diocese of Ardagh and Clonmacnois.

Useful Guides to Administrative Divisions

To use the full range of records, it will be necessary to place ancestral locations within the different divisions noted above. This may be complicated by variations in place-names which occur between different record sources. The sources below are useful in locating places, and in finding name variations. They may provide leads to other sources, and these opportunities are specified in each case.

Ordnance Survey Field Name Books (1830s)
The Ordnance Survey Field Name Books are notebooks used by the surveyors compiling the first Ordnance Survey in the 1830s. They are arranged by civil parish and townland and describe the land type, land-holders names and often a drawing of the houses.

A Topographical Dictionary of Ireland by Samuel Lewis (London 1837).
This very informative guide, originally published in three volumes, lists
all civil parishes, major market towns and some villages in alphabetical
order. Each entry contains a brief account of the town or parish listed,
and a summary of economic and social conditions. A brief description
of both Catholic and non-Catholic parishes is provided together with a
list of public buildings and major local landowners. The third volume
is an atlas and features maps of each county. Lewis's Topographical
Dictionary of Ireland is available on line at www.libraryireland.com
and in hardcopy in most major libraries.

RATHGRAFF, or CASTLE-POLLARD, a parish,
in the barony of DEMIFORE, county of WESTMEATH,
and province of LEINSTER, on the road from Dublin
to Granard, and on the river Glore; containing, with
the post-town of Castle-Pollard, 3612 inhabitants.
This parish, also called Rathgarth and Rathgarrue,
comprises 5181¾ statute acres of land, chiefly arable and producing good crops: limestone abounds,
for working which there are some large quarries:
there is very little bog. Within the parish are the
hills of Sliebuoy and Loughanstown. Fairs for live
stock are held at Castle-Pollard, and petty sessions
every Wednesday. Kinturk is the seat of W. D. Pollard, Esq. The living is a vicarage, in the diocese of
Meath, united by act of council, in 1676, to the vicar-
ages of Lickbla, Faughley and Mayne, and to the cu-
racies of St. Feighan-of-Fore, Favoran, Beatæ-Mariæ-
de-Fore, and Kilpatrick, forming the union of Rathgraff,
in the patronage of the Bishop; the rectory is impropriate in the Marquess of Westmeath. The tithes
amount to £187. 9., of which £83. 6. 3½. is payable to
the impropriator; the gross value of the benefice is
£609. 11. 4., including £42, the value of 31 acres com-
prised in three glebes. The glebe-house is a good com-
fortable building in Castle-Pollard. The church is a
handsome building, surmounted with a spire, in the
C........ .... in excellent repair, having been rebuilt
.... a loan from the late

An extract from *A Topographical Dictionary of Ireland*
see above

Parliamentary Gazetteer of Ireland (1844/45)

This provides similar information to Lewis's Topographical Dictionary of Ireland for a slightly later period, and includes a more detailed account of the heritage, social and trading conditions. It is available for reference in most major libraries.

KILBEGGAN, a parish, containing a town of the same name, in the barony of Moycashel, co. Westmeath, Leinster. Length, 4 miles; breadth, 3¼; area, 6,085 acres, 3 roods, 26 perches. Pop., in 1831, 4,039; in 1841, 4,186. Houses 755. Pop., of the rural districts, in 1831, 2,054; in 1841, 2,276. Houses 412. The surface is tame in character, and comprises a considerable extent of bog; yet consists, in the aggregate, of good land. The Upper Brosna effects the drainage southward; the great Connaught road from Dublin passes westward; and a branch of the Grand Canal comes up to the town from the main line on the south. The chief country-seats are Meeldrum, Loughangore, and Belmont. The highest ground is at the church, and lies only 251 feet above sea-level.—This parish is a perpetual curacy, and a separate benefice, in the dio. of Meath. Glebe, £33 12s. 8d. Gross income, £212 16s.; nett, £92 19s. 1d. Patron, the diocesan. The tithes are wholly impropriate in Sir Lambart Cromie, bart., and have been compounded for £150. The church was built in 1764, at an unknown cost, and repaired in 1818, by means of a loan of £461 10s. 9¼d., from the late Board of First Fruits. Sittings 200; attendance, from 80 to 95. The Roman Catholic chapel has an attendance of 2,500; and, in the Roman Catholic parochial arrangement, is united to the chapel of Rahue. In 1834, the parishioners consisted of 253 Churchmen, 15 Protestant dissenters, and 3,841 Roman Catholics; and 7 pay daily schools had on their books 142 boys and 98 girls. In 1840, a male school and a female school in the town, were salaried with respectively £12 and £8 from the National Board.

An entry from *Parliamentary Gazetteer of Ireland* - see above.

An Index to Townlands & Towns, Parishes & Baronies of Ireland (1851).
Commonly referred to as the 'Townland Index', this is a full alphabetical
listing of all Townlands, Towns, Civil Parishes and Baronies of Ireland.
It was prepared for administration of each census, and the one usually
used is the 1851 edition. It is indexed by townland, and also by Parish
and Barony. The townland section identifies the Barony, Parish and Poor
Law Union in which each is situated. It also provides a reference to
locate the townland on Ordnance Survey Maps. Originally published by
Thoms (Dublin) it has been republished by the Genealogical Publishing
Co. (Baltimore), 1984 and others (see page 27).

1885. Townlands in Poor Law Unions
This publication lists the townlands within the Superintendent Registrar's
District of each county. It is divided into Poor Law Unions, each of
which is arranged by District Electoral Division (DED) and then by Civil
Parish. It is very useful for identifying neighbouring townlands in a Civil
Parish and establishing the correct spelling or an alternative spelling
of a townland. It was compiled by George B. Handran, from 'Lists of
Townlands in Poor Law Unions' dated 1885 and later. It was published
by Higginson (USA, 1997). All the Poor Law Unions for Westmeath
are dated 1885, except Tullamore which is dated 1905.

General Topographical Index to Townlands and Towns of Ireland (1901)
This index is similar to the 1851 Index, but also lists the DED name
and number which is important when checking administrative records.
Both of these titles are available for reference in most libraries.

Irish Historic Maps
A local tax or rating system was introduced as a result of the Irish Poor
Relief act of 1838. For this purpose all property had to be mapped
and valued. The resulting maps on a scale of 6 inches to 1 mile were
officially called The Townland Survey of Ireland. The beautifully
illustrated maps show locations for buildings, farms, cemeteries,
churches, schools, hospitals, etc. The 1838 maps for County Westmeath,
and more recent maps for the period 1888 to 1913, are available on line
at www.osi.ie/publicviewer

Number of the Sheet of the Ordnance Survey Maps.	Townlands and Towns.	Area in Statute Acres. A. R. P.	County.	Barony.	Parish.	Poor Law Union in 1857.	Townland Census of 1851, Part I. Vol. Page
38	Kiltober	380 2 20	Westmeath	Moycashel	Rahugh	Tullamore	I. 279
38	Kiltober and Grange	296 3 29	Westmeath	Moycashel	Kilbeggan	Tullamore	I. 278
27	Kiltaghert	813 3 23a	Leitrim	Leitrim	Kiltoghert	Car¹. on Shannon	IV. 102
27	KILTOGHERT T.	—	Leitrim	Leitrim	Kiltoghert	Car¹. on Shannon	IV. 103
21	Kiltogurra	305 0 33	Mayo	Kilmaine	Cong	Ballinrobe	IV. 104
,70	Kiltole	307 1 11	Donegal	Raphoe	Raphoe	Strabane	III. 141
1	Kiltomuly	167 3 16	Cavan	Tullyhaw	Killinagh	Enniskillen	III. 92
15	Kiltomy	177 1 11	Kerry	Clanmaurice	Kiltony	Listowel	II. 172
9	Kiltoulig	357 1 12	Cork, E.R.	Orrery and Kilmore	Ballyhay	Kilmallock	II. 104
,48	Kiltoom	115 0 34	Roscommon	Athlone	Kiltoom	Athlone	IV. 183
7	Kiltoom	836 3 28	Westmeath	Fore	Faughalstown	Granard	I. 270
,36	Kiltoome	179 1 10	Meath	Upper Navan	Kilcooly	Trim	I. 216
73	Kiltooris	192 3 33b	Donegal	Boylagh	Inishkeel	Glenties	III. 113
32	Kiltorcan	976 3 32	Kilkenny	Knocktopher	Derrynahinch	Thomastown	I. 111
99	Kiltormer East	406 3 12	Galway	Longford	Kiltormer	Ballinasloe	IV. 60
99	KILTORMER T.		Galway	Longford	Kiltormer	Ballinasloe	IV. 60
99	Kiltormer West	196 2 31	Galway	Longford	Kiltormer	Ballinasloe	IV. 60
39	Kiltotan and Collinstown	328 1 36	Westmeath	Fartullagh	Castlelost	Mullingar	I. 268

Entries from 'General Alphabetical Index to the Townlands and Towns, Parishes and Baronies of Ireland (1851)
- see page 26

HEN—HEW]   **INDEX to**

Name and Registration District.	Vol.	Page
HENSON, Christopher. Athlone	3	7
—— Joseph. Athlone	3	8
—— Patrick. Athlone	3	2
HENSTON, Charles Copeman. Tipperary	3	723
HENSY, Daniel. Belfast	16	268
—— Thomas. Borrisokane	13	411
HENTHORN, Thomas. Cootehill	8	193
HENUE, Stephen. Clifden	4	229
HENVEY, John. Balrothery	12	431
HENWOOD, Thomas Charles. Ballycastle	16	71
HENY, Martin Joseph. Galway	19	269
HENZY, John. Mountmellick	18	513
HEOGARTY, George Albert. Cork	10	127
HEPENSTALL, Dora Frances. Rathdrum	7	1019
—— William. Dublin, South	12	634
HEPES, Elizabeth. Trim	2	1064
HEPPENSTALL, Jane. New Ross	19	818
HEPSTON, Morris. Dublin, South	2	793
HERAGHTY, Bridget. Dunfanaghy	2	62
—— Catherine. Westport	9	576
—— Catherine. Westport	4	645
—— Denis. Dunfanaghy	17	65
—— Hannah. Dunfanaghy	17	62
—— Hugh. Dunfanaghy	2	60
—— James. Dunfanaghy	12	55
—— James. Millford	17	251
—— James. Sligo	17	305
—— John. Sligo	12	314
—— John. Dunfanaghy	12	52
—— John. Dunfanaghy	7	68
—— Mary. Dunfanaghy	2	67
—— Mary. Millford	17	253
—— Michael. Sligo	12	314
—— Michael. Sligo	12	-314
—— Michael. Sligo	7	337
—— Patrick. Dunfanaghy	2	60
—— Patrick. Dunfanaghy	2	62
—— Thomas. Westport	19	567

Entries from the
Index to Births Registered in Ireland, 1877

Chapter 4   Civil Registration

One of the largest and most valuable sources available to the family history researcher is the civil register of birth, marriage and death held by the General Register Office (www.groireland.ie). This organisation is now located in Roscommon, but has a local office in Dublin. Civil registration began in Ireland in 1845 with the recording of non Catholic marriages. It was not until 1864 that registration of all marriages, and of births and deaths commenced.

Registration was administered within registration districts which are geographically identical to the Poor Law Union (see page 18). Copies of these local records were then transferred to the General Register Office (GRO) which held all national records (See Chapter 15).There is currently one registration office in Westmeath and this is located in Mullingar.

The reporting of births to a local registrar was the duty of family members or friends as hospitals were only available to a small minority until well into the 20th century. The reporting of deaths was also the duty of family members or friends unless the death occurred in hospital, often the workhouse infirmary (available to local residents as well as inmates of the workhouse). Undoubtedly some events were not recorded. The Registration of marriages, on the other hand, was the responsibility of the cleric conducting the marriage. The following records are held at the General Register Office:

Births

Birth records specify date and place of birth; name of child; name and dwelling place of father; name and maiden surname of mother; occupation of father; qualification and residence of informant; and date registered. The informant is the person who registered the birth, and is generally a family member or, on rare occasions, a midwife (see page 31).

Marriages

Non-Catholic marriage records are available from 1845 and all marriages from 1864. The certificate specifies place and date of marriage; names, ages, condition (i.e. bachelor, spinster, widow etc); residence at time of marriage (valuable information which may lead to further leads); and occupations of bride and groom. The names and occupations of the fathers of the bride and groom (stating 'deceased' if appropriate) and the names of the witnesses are also specified. The ages of the bride or groom are often stated as 'full age', i.e. over 21 years of age (see page 32).

Deaths

Deaths are recorded from 1864 and specify date and place of death; name; marital status; age at the time of death; occupation; cause of death; signature, qualification and residence of the informant and date registered.

Indexes to the Records

All of the records are fully indexed and the website of the General Register Office (GRO) www.groireland.ie details the archive and the terms and conditions relating to searching and obtaining copies (See also page 149). The early indices are bound yearly in a single volume, arranged alphabetically by surname. From 1878 they are divided into four quarterly sections i.e. March (January to March), June (April to June), September (July to September) and December (October to December) which are bound in one or two volumes. If a birth was registered late it is recorded at the back of the index, or possibly in successive years. The indices specify name, registration district and volume and page in the register (see page 28). This information is required in order to purchase a photocopy of the registration entry. The birth indices for the period from 1902 to 1926 include the maiden surname of the mother.

No. (1.)	Date and Place of Birth. (2.)	Name (if any). (3.)	Sex. (4.)	Name and Surname and Dwelling-place of Father. Name and Surname and Maiden Surname of Mother. (5.) (6.)	Rank or Profession of Father. (7.)	Signature, Qualification, and Residence of Informant. (8.)	When Registered. (9.)	Signature of Registrar. (10.)	Baptismal Name if added after Registration of Birth, and Date. (11.)

The registration of birth of the Internationally renowned Irish Tenor, John McCormack at Mardyke Street, Athlone in 1884

18*82* Marriage solemnized at the Roman Catholic Chapel of *Milltown* in the Registrar's District of *Ballynacargy*
in the Union of *Milltown* in the County of *Westmeath*

No. (1.)	When Married. (2.)	Name and Surname. (3.)	Age. (4.)	Condition. (5.)	Rank or Profession. (6.)	Residence at the Time of Marriage. (7.)	Father's Name and Surname. (8.)	Rank or Profession of Father. (9.)
57	Thirty first July 1882	John Murtagh	29 years	Bachelor	farmer	Corrolly Parish of Street	William Murtagh	farmer
		Mary Drew	24 years	Spinster	Daughter of a farmer	Baltisfoot Empor	James Drew	farmer

Married in the Roman Catholic Chapel of *Milltown* according to the Rites and Ceremonies of the Roman Catholic Church by me, *P. Gallaghan*

This Marriage was solemnized between us,	John Murtagh	in the Presence of us,	Patrick Murtagh
	Mary Drew		Kate Drew

Civil registration entry for the marriage of John Murtagh and Mary Drew in July 1882

Practical Points to Remember

A few practical points to remember in searching this source are:

- Family names may not be spelled in the same way as they are now, e.g. O'Connor may be Connor or Connors; variants of a name may therefore need to be checked.

- The information on the certificates was supplied by whoever registered the event and may not always be totally correct.

- Ages recorded on marriage and death records should not be taken as accurate. Ages specified on marriage records are the prerogative of the bride and groom and may vary for predictable reasons of vanity or legality. The age on a death record should be treated with caution, particularly where the informant is not a family member; although stated ages will generally be close to the actual age, errors of up to 10 years, are not uncommon in deaths of older people.

- If a child's name had not been decided at the time of birth registration, 'male' or 'female' will be entered in the name column.

- Note also that the indices are based on the date of registration and not the date on which the event occurred. It is not unknown for a long period of time to elapse before registration took place. It may therefore be necessary to search for several years after the supposed date of an event to find a record. Events recorded more than a year late are usually included in the Late Registrations section at the back of each annual volume but occasionally appear in the body of the volume, in which case there will be no indication in the index of the actual date of death.

Other Civil Registration Records

Other records held at the GRO that may have relevance to Westmeath:

- Births at sea of children one of whose parents was born on the island of Ireland from 1864.
- Deaths at sea of persons born on the island of Ireland from 1864.
- Births of children of Irish parents, certified by British Consuls abroad, from 1864.
- Deaths of Irish-born persons, certified by British Consuls abroad from 1864.

Access to GRO Records

In addition to the GRO itself (www.groireland.ie), indices to the GRO records may be accessed at the following archives:

LDS Family History Centre

Church of Jesus Christ of Latter Day Saints (LDS) family history centre holdings. The International Genealogical Index (IGI) includes copies of GRO Indices from 1864, (1845 in the case of non-Catholic marriages); Indices to 1958 are available online, without charge, at www.familysearch.org; they may be searched by full name, surname or even forename (useful in the case of an unusual forename), and the search engine will search for name variants. It may be useful to search this source for possible dates before conducting a search of the GRO index. The LDS holdings available online also include copies of entries from 1864 to about 1880 (See Page 152).

IGI Individual Record	FamilySearch™ International Genealogical Index v5.0
	British Isles

JAMES O'DALY   Pedigree
  Male

Event(s):
  Birth: 1686 Ballinderry, , , Westmeath, Ireland
  Christening:
  Death: 21 JAN 1759
  Burial:

Parents:
  Father: EDMUND O'DALY   Family
  Mother: ROSE LEDVIGE

Messages:
Form submitted by a member of the LDS Church. The form lists the submitter's name and address and may include source information. The address may be outdated. Details vary. To find the form, you must know the batch and sheet number.

Source Information:
  Batch Number: 7909391
  Sheet: 87
  Source Call No.: 1260516   **Type:** Film

An entry from the IGI database at www.familysearch.org

Dublin City Library and Archive
Dublin City Library and Archive also holds IGI microfilm copies of the
LDS indices to births, marriages and deaths.

National Library of Ireland
1. Index to births for the years 1864, 1865 and 1866 (Ref: LB Thom
3121) These are bound volume copies of those held by the GRO
Research Room in Dublin.

2. Index to deceased seamen from 1887 to 1949.
Names of seamen whose deaths were reported to the GRO providing
the following details: name of deceased; age; rank or profession;
official number; name and type of ship; port of registry; cause; place
and date of death. From 1893 it includes; sex, nationality or place of
birth and last place of abode. (NLI 31242 d).

3. British Armed Forces, Registration of Births, Deaths and Marriages
(from 1761):-
Records of births of children of officers and men of the British
Army etc are available from 1761. Many Irishmen, including
Irish Catholics, joined the British Army. Records of marriages and
deaths are available from 1796. These records are invaluable as
they predate Civil Registration for the wider population and include
events occurring outside Ireland. The records are held at the UK
General Register Office. Indices for 1761 to 1924 may be searched
online at the subscription site www.findmypast.co.uk.

1870-1888. Biths and Marriages of Boggagh
Some 77 entries written by John Galvin of Boggagh, near Moate giving
dates of births, marriages, deaths and emigration. Irish Anc. Vol.4 (1)
1972 pp.21-22

History

A history of civil registration in Ireland was published in 2005, titled,
'Registering the People - 150 Years of Civil Registration' . It is also
available at www.groireland.ie/history.htm

CANVASSING BOOK

No on Register	NAME	RESIDENCE	FOR	AGST
221	Madden, John	Church-street		
222	Madden, James	Wentworth-street		
223	Magauley, James	Loughandoning		
224	Malone, Denis	Dublingate street		
225	Marchbank, James	Mardyke street		
226	Marsh, William	Irishtown		
227	Martin, James	Church street		
228	Martin, William	,,		
229	Maxwell, Patrick	,,		
230	Merrick, James M.	Shamble lane		
231	Mills, John	Connaught-street		
232	Monahan, Rev John	Ballymahon Road		
233	MonahanRevMartin	Ball Alley Lane		
234	Monahan, Michael	Connaught-street		
235	Moore, Patrick	High-street		
236	Moore, John	Irishtown		
237	Moran, Michael	Church street		
238	Moran, Michael	Dublingate street		
239 ✓	Moynan, Thomas	Irishtown		
240	Muldoon, John	Strand street		

(courtesy of Westmeath County Library)

A page from the *Athlone Canvassing Book 1868*
- see page 52

Chapter 5   Censuses and Census Substitutes

As early Irish census records were destroyed for one reason or another, complete official returns are not available prior to the 1901 census. However, a range of other sources may be used to locate individuals within districts. These sources, generally called 'census substitutes', comprise a wide range of records that contain names and other details of the people of Westmeath. These were compiled for a wide range of purposes including administration of land, trade, courts etc. This chapter lists these sources in chronological order.

Official government censuses, recording the names and details of each person in the household, were conducted in Ireland from 1821. This is 20 years before similarly detailed censuses were conducted in England and Wales. Such a census was first attempted in Ireland in 1813 but was not completed. However, the detailed census returns (i.e. the records from each household) of 1821, 1831, 1841 and 1851, together with the surviving returns from 1813, were tragically lost as a result of an explosion and fire in the Public Record Office, located in the Four Courts, in June 1922 during the Civil War.

The returns for 1861 and 1871 were destroyed by government order shortly after each of those censuses were completed. Those for 1881 and 1891 were pulped during the First World War when paper was in short supply. Fragments of the 1821, 1841 and 1851 censuses survive for some counties but none for Westmeath.

The 1901 (see page 52) and 1911(see page 54) censuses are available on line at www.nationalarchives.ie and are on microfilm at the National Archives of Ireland (NAI) and Westmeath Library (WL).

The 'census substitutes' available for Westmeath are as follows:

1640 Irish Proprietors in Moate and District

"Irish Proprietors in Moate and District." Liam Cox, Moate, Co. Westmeath; A History of the Town and District, Athlone, 1981, Appendix 11.

1641 Books of Survey and Distribution

During the Cromwellian plantation of the 1650s land was confiscated from those who owned it prior to the rebellion of 1641 and distributed to new owners. The latter were mainly soldiers in the parliamentary armies, or adventurers who had provided financial backing to the English Parliament for their armies. This book details the distribution of forfeited land under the Acts of Settlement and Explanation 1662. It summarises all the changes that took place in landownership from 1640 to the end of the 1600s. It is arranged by name of occupier, townland and acreage. It lists the names of pre-1640 land-owners and of the new owners after the plantations. Those listed are large landholders and this limits its use as a genealogical tool to the greater portion of the population. However, it does point one in the direction of relevant estate papers. Note that townland names in this record may be spelled differently from what appears in land records of the 1800s. The Books of survey and distribution of the estates in the County of Westmeath, forfeited in the year 1641 is available on microfilm at the NAI Ref MFS 02F/7, the NLI, Ms 966, The Royal Irish Academy, Ms.H. II.2. A printed version (J.C. Lyons, Ladiston, 1852) which includes a general index is available on CD and microfilm at WL. For further information on the variant copies of the Books of survey and distribution for Westmeath see Geraldine Tallon, 'Books of Survey and Distribution, Co. Westmeath', Analecta Hibernica, 28, 1978, pp 105-115.

1659 A Census of Ireland

A Census of Ireland Circa 1659 with supplementary material from the Poll Money Ordinances (1660-1661) compiled by Sir William Petty (Ed. Séamus Pender, Dublin 1939) is a listing of those liable to pay Poll Tax. It gives information under the following headings; Parishes, Townlands, Number of People, Tituladoes Names (meaning men of title or standing) English or Irish. It also shows the principal Irish families appearing in each barony and their number. William J. Smyth in his introduction to the new edition of A Census of Ireland Circa 1659 gives an excellent analysis of the census and its use as a data source.

1665 Hearth Money Rolls

The Hearth Money Rolls is a listing of all those liable to pay a tax based on the number of hearths (i.e. fireplaces) in each house. The original was destroyed in the fire in the Public Records Office in 1922, however a copy transcribed in 1909 by Sean O Fairceallaigh survived. "The Hearth Money Roll, 1665 for Mullingar" transcribed by John Brady is published in The Franciscan College Annual June, 1950. This publication is available to researchers at the NLI Ref Ir 37941 f3 and WL. A Hearth Money Roll giving Protestants and Papists in Athlone town (1724?) is in the Public Records Office Northern Ireland (PRONI) Ref. T.1023 (245).

1699 Jacobite Outlaws

Approx 300 names and townland addresses of landholders outlawed as Jacobites (followers of James II). Anal Hib. 22 (1960) 11-230. - see illustration below

COUNTY WESTMEATH [third list]

Thomas Nugent, Clovin [Clonin], esq, otherwise called Thomas, earl of Westmeath

Alexander M'Donnell alias Gregor alias Boyd, do, esq.

James Nugent, Donore, esq

Christopher Nugent, Clonlenny, esq

Michael Dardis, Gigginstowne, gent

James Dardis, do, gent

John Nugent, Teighmon alias Tagmont, bt

Richard Nugent, do, esq

John Nugent, Killagh, gent

1702-03 Land Acquisitions

Alphabetical list of those acquiring land in Westmeath. RIA (Upton Papers, No. 4); SLC film 101011.

1704 - 1839 Convert Rolls

This is a listing of Catholics who renounced (or pretended to renounce) their faith in order to hold on to their estates during Penal times. A Calendar of Convert Rolls Vol. 1. 1703-89 and Vol. II 1789-1845 is held at the NAI. A microfilm copy is held at the NLI, P.1898. Lists of Converts, 1702-1772, and Protestant settlers in Ireland from 1662 to 1772 is held at the British Museum in London, Egerton Ms.77. A microfilm copy is held at the NLI, P.1357. Also *'The Convert Rolls'* edited by Eileen O'Byrne (With Fr Wallace Clare's annotated list of converts, 1703-78 edited by Anne Chamney) Dublin, Irish Manuscripts Commission, 2005.

1731 Rathaspick Protestants

Census of Protestants in Shrule and Rathreagh (Longford) and Rathaspick (Westmeath). RCB Library GS 2/7/3/25

1741 Westmeath Survey

A Survey of County Westmeath. Dublin: Royal Irish Academy, Ms. H I 1.

1749 Census of Elphin

Bishop Edward Synge of Elphin carried out a census of his diocese (which includes parts of Westmeath) in 1749 to establish the proportion of Roman Catholics and Protestants. It includes the heads of households and lists: name, townland, religion, profession, and numbers of children under and over fourteen years, and of men servants and women servants. It is available in the NAI and has been published by the Irish Manuscripts Commission, Dublin, 2004 as *The Census of Elphin 1749*, edited by Marie-Louise Legg. It is available on line by subscription at www.irishorigins.com.

1761 Poll Book

Co. Westmeath Poll Book (a list of voters) NLI, GO Ms. 443; SLC mf. 100181.

Nugent, Robert, of Earl Street, cert. 10 October 1778, enrolled 13 October 1778 (A).

Nugent, Susanna Cath., called Lady Riverston, cert. 5 May 1732, enrolled 17 June 1732 (A). Nugent, Mrs Susanne-Catherine, of Dublin, called Lady Riverston, conformity 21 December 1731 (B). (D).

Nugent, Mr Thomas, Donora, Co Westmeath, cert. and enrolled 20 May 1734 (A). Conformity 19 May 1734 (B). Esq. (D).

Nugent, Right Honourable Thomas, Earl of Westmeath, cert. 12 August 1754, enrolled 13 August 1754 (A). See Westmeath, Thomas.

Nugent, William, Esq., commonly called Lord Riverston, Dublin, cert. 1 February 1738, enrolled 3 February 1738 (A). Conformity 28 January 1738 (B). (D).

Nugent, William, of Street, Co Westmeath, cert. 14 February 1782, enrolled 20 February 1782 (A).

Nugent, William, of Chancery Hill, Co Westmeath, cert. and enrolled 12 June 1782 (A).

Nunan, James of Ardmore, cert. 9 June 1781, enrolled 15 November 1781 (A).

Nunan, Philip. See Nugent, Philip.

O'Berne, John, Esq., cert. 20 September 1782, enrolled 5 October 1782 (A).

O'Brien, Anastatia, of KillmcDonald in Co Limerick, cert. 2 December 1775, enrolled 4 December 1775 (A). [Bracketed with Mathew O'Brien].

O'Brien, Ann, d. Cashel, cert. 12 October 1765, enrolled 25 November 1765 (A). Conformity 18 August 1765 (B). (D).

O'Brien, Catherine, cert. 7 September 1772, enrolled 10 September 1772 (A). D. Lismore, conformity 30 August 1772 (B).

O'Brien, Charles, of the parish of Cahirconlish, cert. 15 November 1784, enrolled 20 November 1784 (A).

O'Brien, Christopher, gent., Dublin, cert. 16 November 1714, enrolled 17 November 1714 (A). O'Bryan, Christopher, d. Dublin, conformity 12 November 1714 (B). (C).

Extract from
'The Convert Rolls' by Eileen O'Byrne (IMC, Dublin 1981)
showing those who converted from Catholicism to the Church of Ireland between 1703 and 1789. Each entry shows the date on which the convert was certified (cert.) as having attended a Church of Ireland service, and also the date on which they were formally enrolled as a Church of Ireland member. Note that many people registered themselves as being 'of Dublin' so as to hide their identity.

1761 Land Survey and Voters

A book of survey of all the land in the County of Westmeath, early 18th c?, and a list of voters at a poll to elect Members of Parliament, May 11, 1761. NLI, Mss.2296-2297.

1761-88 *Owners of Freeholds in Co. Westmeath.*

Compiled for Electoral Purposes. 1761 – 1788. NLI mss. 787-788. (A Freeholder was a person who held land for the duration of his life or for lives specified).

1762-77 *Barronstown Rent Book*

Barronstown (sic) estate. 1st November 1762 – 1st May 1777. Rent book for the estate of the Honourable Anthony Malone, Barronstown (near Ballynacarrigy), Co. Westmeath. WL Ref. P/M/D

1766 *Russough Religious Census*

Religious Census of the Parish of Russough, NAI/M2476(e) NLI G.O. Ms No. 537

1786 *Westmeath Register of Trees*

Under legislation to halt destruction of Irish woods, those planting trees were required to give notice. Includes names of landowners who planted trees. Microfilm copy available WL - see page 43.

1796 *Flax Growers*

This is a listing of flax growers in the 1790s who were eligible for a prize of a spinning wheel from the Linen Board. It is available at www.failteromhat.com/flax1796, also at the NAI, Microfiches No. 1-12 and in the Main Reading Room of the NLI, Ir 300 s 21.

1798 *Claimants and Surrenders of the Rebellion*

The 1798 Rebellion was a traumatic period and lists of those who claimed compensation for loss of property during this Rebellion have been compiled by Ian Cantwell and published on CD (Eneclann, 2005). It specifies name, residence, county, place where loss was sustained and nature of loss. There are 48 entries for Westmeath. Indices of surnames, places and occupations are available online at http://www.iancantwell.com

from the 1786 *Westmeath Register of Trees* - see page 42

(Courtesy of Westmeath County Library)

1802-03 Census of Protestants
Census of Protestants in the Parishes of Ballyloughloe, Castletown Delvin, Clonarney, Drumraney, Enniscoffey, Kilbridepass, Killallon, Kilcleagh, Killough, Killua, Killucan, Leney, Moyliscar, and Rathconnell." Ir. Anc. 5 (2) (1973): 120-26. (see page 45).

1806-1808 Corkree Infantry
Roll of Corkree Infantry NLI Ms. 8733

1814 Major Landholders
Major landholders of Westmeath (alphabetical by townland). RIA (Upton Papers, No. 4); SLC film 1010011.

1820 – 1957 Transatlantic Passenger Lists
Lists of passengers from Ireland to various American ports are available online at the subscription site www.ancestry.com.

1821-1850 Register of Castlepollard Fever Hospital
Information recorded under the following headings: When admitted: patients name: place of abode: diseases: died or cured: when died or discharged. NLI Ref. P.4067. Transcribed by Micheál Ó Conláin, [Mullingar], 1998, (typescript)WL.

1822 Illicit Distillation
A return of 22 of persons tried for illicit distillation at Mullingar Lent assizes, 1822. NAI CSO/RP/1822/3392/9

1824-35 Tithe Applotment Books (see page 82).

1829 Freeholders
Notices of applications for registering freeholds. The Westmeath Journal, May 1829 (see page 110)

1831-37 Freemen of Athlone
(approximately 170 names, addresses, and occupations.) Parl. Papers 1837, 11 (1): Appendix B1; 1837/38,13 (2): Appendix 3.

1832 Westmeath Voters
Those who applied for a vote in 1832. Lists the applicant's name, place of residence, property value, name of landlord and date and place of registry. Baronies of Brawney – Clonlonan, Kilkenny West,

Frances, Francis infant. BRENNAN John, wife Mary, Eliz. 14, Mary 12, Frances 9. CUNNINGHAM James, wife Hester, Ann 4, Peter 1, Sarah 1, SMITH Eliz. 12. CONNER Mary widow, John, William, Henry, Charles, Mary. CONNER Esther widow, William, Charles, Eleanor, GRIMES Eliz. SCOTT William servant to Earl of Granard, wife Mary do., William 14, Mary 13, Selina 9, QUIN Philadelphia servant to Earl of Granard.

LACKEN PARISH
DELAMAS Peter, CARROLL Mary servant.

TYFARNAN PARISH
MITCHEL John, wife Mary. MITCHEL Thomas, wife Ann, Catherine 13, Thomas 10, Francis 7, William 6, Stewart 5, Ann 3, Mary Ann 2, Eliz. 1.

KILMACNEVAN PARISH
RAY Charles, wife R.C., William, John, Adam 13, Charles 1. MURDOW Joseph, wife Isabella, Mary, Sarah 15, William 14, Eliz. 9, Isabella 7, Joseph 4. COWEN Ann widow, William, wife R.C., Mary 13, Ann 9, Eliz. 7, Catherine 3. KIRK Mary widow, DODD Mary widow. MEARES Hannah, Ann, Mary.

TEMPLEORAN PARISH
TUITE Sir Henry, Lady, seldom resident, Hugh, wife Sarah, Henry 11, Hugh 9, George 7, Melusina 5, BROTHERSON Richard, wife Mary Ann servants, HOWE Ann. BRABAZON William, wife Jane, John 12, Robert 10, Ann 6, William 3, Jane infant. AUSTIN Samuel, wife Eliz., John 9, Eleanor 7, Alice 5, William 3, George 1. ORR Samuel, wife Ann, Mary 10, Margaret 5, Diana 3. SHAW Richard, wife Mary, WILSON Margaret. AUSTIN John, Jane, Sarah. THOMPSON Ann widow, Eleanor, John.
(*Note: The following persons reside on a townland which pays tithe to Sir John Pierse and county taxes as belonging to the Parish of Dysart, therefore, according to the decision of the late Lord Kilwarden in a similar case which occurred in the Parish of Tyfarnam at the last Spring Assizes, they are to be considered as inhabitants of Templeoran*)
MATHEWS George, wife Hannah, George, John, David, Mary. SHERMAN John, wife Mary, Robert, Thomas, James, Catherine, Ann, Sarah. SHERMAN William, wife Ann. RAY John, wife Ann, John, wife Mary, Ann 2. RAY Patrick, wife R.C., John 4, Mary 1. RAY Benjamin, Robert, John, Ann.

PARISH OF MOYLISCAR — Thomas Robinson, Vicar, May 1803
(*Head of household, number in family male and female, number of servants and tenants male and female*)
BELVEDERE Earl of, 1, 0, 1, 3. ROCHFORT Gustavus Esq 8, 4, 8, 9. ROBINSON Rev. Thomas 2, 3, 15, 19. DENNIS Rev. Meade 6, 5. L'ESTRANGE Rev. Samuel 3, 4, 2, 0. HICKEY Noah Esq 4, 2. JONES David Esq 1, 2, 0, 2. GERRARD Thomas Esq 3, 3. EVANS Francis Esq 4, 2. NIXON John Esq 1, 5. NAYNO Major 3, 3. SWIFT Meade Esq 3, 3. BRIGGS Roger 2, 1. SMYTH Peter 3, 0. BURROWS John 2, 1. STRONG Robert 4, 4. FLETCHER Thomas 1, 1. HANAGAN Thomas 3, 3. FINLAY widow 0, 1.

PARISH OF RATHCONNELL — Francis Pratt Winter, Vicar, August 1802
"*This return was at first drawn up before it was known that it would be necessary to ascertain the age of each individual, which has caused considerable delay, and it has been thought better at length to take the age of some upon common report rather than press the disclosure where it appears disagreeable.*"

REYNELLA
REYNELL Richard 42, wife Eliz. Molesworth 36, Arthur 12, Richard 9, Francis 8, BURN Anna Maria 47, MAXWELL John 40 servants.

An extract from an 1802-3 Census of Protestants published in the *Irish Ancestor* - see page 44.

CLONLONAN AND BRAWNY BARONY.

Names.	Place of Abode.	Situation of Leasehold, Freehold, &c.	Value.	Name of Landlord.	Place and Date of Registry.
Allen, Patrick	Maghernerla	House and Land, Maghernerla	10		Castlepollard, 10th October, 1832.
Adamson, Christopher	Balnalack	Ditto Balnalack	50		ditto ditto
Adamson, Robert	Moate	Land, Tullybane	90		ditto ditto
Allen, George, jun.	Auburne, Athlone	Houses and Land, Kilnacough	10		Moate, 2d November, 1832
Barlow, John Thomas	Moate	Houses and Land, Moate	50		Castlepollard, 11th October, 1832
Burns, Lawford	do	Ditto Aughennrgit	20		ditto ditto
Boswell, John	Athlone	Lands, Mornashill	50		ditto ditto
Bruce, John	Auburne	House and Land, Auburne	50		Moate, 27th October, 1832
Boswell, William	Athlone	Houses and Lands, Athlone	50		ditto ditto
Bigley, Joseph	Cranagh, Co. Roscommon	Land, Carnemady	10		ditto ditto
Clibborn, Cuthbert John	Moate	Lands, Moate	50		Castlepollard, 12th October, 1832.
Claffy, James	Bogagh	House and Land, Bogagh	10		Moate, 29th October, 1832.
Daly, Joseph Morgan	Castledaly	Lands, Castledaly	50		Mullingar, 15th October, 1832
Dillon, John Christopher	Athlone	Houses and Land, Clonbrusk	20		Moate, 29th October, 1832.
Dillon, Christopher	do	Lands, Curragh, Grimes field, Robinson's field, Lough-inaskill, and Acrequarries	20		ditto ditto
Dillon, Chas. Henry	do	Houses and Concerns, North Gate-street, Athlone	20		Mullingar, 16th November, 1832.

From a list of *Westmeath Voters in 1832* - see page 44.

Moycashel and Rathconrath. Ir. Gen. 5, (2) (1975); pp. 234-49: continued in 6 (1): pp. 90-98; Corkaree, Delvin, Demifore, and Farbill. Ir. Gen. 5, (6) (1979): pp. 772-89; Fartullagh, Moycashel and Magherdernan, and Moygoise. Ir. Gen. 6, (1) (1980) pp. 77-98. These lists are also available on CD-ROM at WL.

1832 – 36 Liquor Licences

List of Holders of, or Applicants for, Licenses to Sell Liquor in Athlone. (over 100 names and addresses). Parl. Papers 1837, 13 (2): Appendix 10.

1835 Census of the Parish of Killcumreagh (Tubber)

Gives name, male/female, age, head, occupation, and Catholic/Protestant/Dissenter in each townland. Published in A Pre-Famine Survey of Kilcrumreragh: a unique social document of Rosemount, Jeremiah Sheehan and Fr. Jimmy Murray, printed by Westmeath Examiner, Mullingar, [1997]. Microfilm copy of original is available in NLI. Ref. P. 1994.

Name	Female	Age	Head	Calling	Catholic	Protestant	Dissenter
Thomas Brennon	"	40	H	Farmer	C		
Bridget Brennon	F	36			C		
Matthew Brennon	"	3			C		
Margaret Brennon	F	8			C		
Mary Brennon	F	5mts			C		
Patrick Creevy	"	38	H	Labourer	C		
Betty Creevy	F	33			C		
Edward Creevy	"	5			C		
David Creevy	"	3			C		
Mary Creevy	F	1			C		
John Dillin	"	28	H	Labourer	C		
Richard Dillin	"	26		Labourer	C		
Catharine Dillin	F	60			C		
Cathal Kennelty	F	23		Servant	C		
John Daley	"	28	H	Labourer	C		
Mary Daley	F	26			C		
Anne Daley	F	12			C		
Kitty Daley	F	23			C		

A page from the *1835 Census of Killcumreagh*

(Courtesy of Fr. Jimmy Murray)

1838 Illiterate Voters

Lists of Marksmen (illiterate voters) in Athlone. 42 names, occupations, and residences. Parl. Papers 1837, 11 (1); Appendix A3; and 1837/38, 13 (2): appendix 4.

1838- 1863 Lowry Estate Rentals

Rental of the estate of Robert William Lowry, Pomeroy House, County Tyrone, giving details of rents paid by named tenants in the Ballymore area of Westmeath 1 Nov 1838 – 24 Nov 1863. WL, REF P/L/E. SLC film1279281.

1840 Westmeath Electors

Westmeath Electors giving name; residence; situation and value of freehold; and indications of political leanings, compiled circa 1840, with additions for period 1840-45. Lists for each Barony are available in; Clonlonan and Brawney NLI Ms. 1454; Corkaree NLI Ms. 1455; Delvin NLI Mss. 1436, 1456; Farbill NLI Ms. 1457; Fartullagh NLI Ms. 1458; Kilkenny West NLI Ms. 1459; Moyashel and Magheradernon NLI Ms. 1460; Moycashel NLI Ms. 1461; Moygoish NLI Ms. 1462; and Rathconrath NLI Mss. 1463, 1402.

1841 – 1911 Censuses of England and Wales

This census required those born outside of England and Wales to enter only the country of birth, eg Ireland or Scotland, rather than the county of birth. However, the county of birth was usually provided by the Irish-born. These censuses are in the UK National Archives, Kew and can be searched online on the subscription sites www.ancestry.co.uk and www.findmypast.co.uk.

1841 – 1911 Censuses of Scotland

As with the above censuses, the county of birth was often provided by Irish-born. The censuses are held at the Scottish National Archives, Edinburgh, but may be searched online on subscription sites www.ancestry.co.uk and www.findmypast.co.uk. Indices may be be searched online at www.scotlandspeople.gov.uk

1842-1854 Clonfad, Castletown Rentals

Rental of the estate of G.A. Boyd of Middleton Park, Castletown. Rentals of 211 properties in Clonfad and surrounding parishes. NLI, Ms. 3108; Mf. WL.

RENTAL of the Estate of GEORGE AUGUSTUS BOYD, Esquire,

No.	Folio.	Denominations.	Tenants' Names.	Arrears due. 1st of ..... 184_	Half-Year's Rent due to May 1852
127	165	Millturn	Tshitt Michael	"	4 14 0
128	186	do	Tshitt Edward	"	2 12 0
129	188	do	Bennett Christopher	"	7 18 3
130	189	do	Byrne Lawrence	"	2 10 0
131	191	do	Byrne Thomas	16 11 6	7 7 3
132	190	do	Byrne Patrick	"	2 10 0
133	192	do	Caddle Widow	"	8 17 11
134	159	do	Caddle Walter	"	11 0 0
135	193	do	Cormick Christopher	9 8	" 9 8
136	194	do	Curan Lawrence	14 4	" 14 4
137	195	do	Coffy Rep. of Revd Bryan	"	43 6 4
138	197	do	Curan Patrick	1 10 0	" 15 6

Tenants from the *Clonfad, Castletown Rentals* - see page 48

1843 Voters List.
NAI 1843/60

1848 William Smith O'Brien Petition
Petitioners for William Smith O'Brien. Names of male petitioners in Clonmellon. NAI 1848/180. Lawler, Ruth, Ed., *The William Smith O'Brien Petition* (CD-ROM), Eneclann, Dublin, 2001.

1850 Inhabitants of Mullingar
In documents relating to sale of Mullingar by Lord Granard to Lord Greville. Includes 1858 Brassington and Gale maps (reproduced in Andrews, J.H., Mullingar Historic Towns Atlas, No.5, Dublin, 1992). Original in archives WL. NLI mf. n.3168, p. 2788. SLC film1279275.

1851-1862 Petty Sessions (Court) Records
Petty session records of those tried for minor crimes in the 'Petty Sessions' courts are available for the court in Athlone (1851-1862, 1894-1910) These are rich resources as they provide names of accused, injured parties and others. Original records are in the NAI and also available on www.findmypast.ie (see page 152).

4		5	6
PARTIES—COMPLAINANT AND DEFENDANT. (The Christian and Surname, Rank, Occupation, or other addition, and Residence, stating Parish and Townland, to be given, and the parties to be distinguished by prefixing their appellation—Complainant or Defendant.)		Names of Witnesses examined, and whether for Complainant or Defendant.	CAUSE OF COMPLAINT, as set forth in Summons.
Complainant.	Defendant.		
James Ryan Const R.I.C.	Thos Geoghegan Clonoion	Const Jones " Ryan	*Drunk 3rd Offence* That Deft was found drunk on the public Street at Athlone on the 9th Jany 1900 - this being his 3rd offence of drunkenness within a period of 12 months
F.W. Jones Const R.I.C.	Wm Mannion Barrybeg	Const Jones Sgt Inglett R.I.C.	*Drunk & disorderly* That Defendant was found drunk and disorderly on the public Street at Athlone on the 16th January 1900
Michl Glynn Const R.I.C	Charles Dolan Cornalee	Const Glynn	*Drunk & disorderly* That Defendant was found drunk and disorderly on the public Street at Athlone on the 16th January 1900

Extract from *Petty Sessions (Court) Records* above
(Courtesy of findmypast.ie)

1854 Griffith's Primary Valuations
See Chapter 7 - Land records.

1854-1865 George Augustus Boyd Rentals
Rental of estates of George Augustus Boyd in Co. Westmeath 1854-1865. NLI, Ms. 1784.

1855 Partial Census of Streete Parish
Census carried out about 1855. NLI Pos. 4236

1861 Athlone Voters
www.igp-web.com/IGPArchives/ire/westmeath/censubs/voters. txt; SLC 1279285 (see below).

Haire, William	Mardyke st.
Handcock, Hon. Robert F.	Northgate st.
Handcock, Hon. Robert John	do.
Handcock, Hon. Richard	do.
Harris, Peter	Mardyke st.
Haughton, Henry	Church st.
Hay, Philip	Fry-place
Hay, William	Victoria place
Hetherington, George	Strand st.
Hoare, Francis	Victoria place
Hogan, Patrick	Castle st
Hogan, William	Irishtown
Holton, John	Fry-place
Holton, William N.	do.
Hopkins, Andrew	King st.
Hopkins, John	Connaught st.
Howe, James	Northgate st.
Huband, Arthur	Court-Devenish
Hughes, Francis	Strand st.
Hynds, John	Queen st
Henry, Patrick	High st.
Hogan, Matthew	Connaught st.
Hynds, Thomas	Irishtown

An extract from *1861 Athlone Voters* - see above.

1863 Rathaspick and Russagh Census
Census of the united parishes of Rathaspick and Russagh. Compiled by Rev. H.W. Stewart, 1863. PRONI, T.2786.

1868-69 Athlone Voters
Canvassing book for Athlone Registry 1868-9. Contains a list of Athlone voters. WL. LS 941.815

1871 Dictionary of Athlone Biography to 1871
Contains the names of inhabitants of the town and neighbourhood and property owners up to 1871. See Burgess Papers page 58.

1873. Names of Workmen on Unidentified Estate
WL Microfilm

1888-95 Rental of Temple Estate
Rental of Temple estate, Waterston, Glasson. 1st May 1888-1st November 1895. Rental of the estate of the Hon. R.T.H. Temple. WL, REF P/T. SLC film 1279275.

c.1892-c.1900. Patrick Coyle's Diary
These notebooks contain comments relating to family history of local people and some pen-and-ink sketches. A typical extract shows: *Mary Smyth of bigwood Frank Smyths Mother died the 23rd of September 1890 a very old woman. If reports can be credited she was born in the year of 1799 her husband Francis Smyth died in February 1870 also her son the Rev. John Smyth departed this life in June 1870 in the city of Adelaide Australia a good pious priest who laboured hard for the Glory of God.* - Copy in WL

1896 Registers of Electors
County wide registers. Registers from 1896-1933 are in the NAI. For those held at the NAI, an advance request must be made to (mail@nationalarchvies.ie) Registers for 1936-37, 1955-56, 1987-88, 1998-99, 2003-05 are available at the NLI. Registers of electors for 1968-69, 1971-72, 1974-75, 1975 onwards are held at WL.

1901 Government of Ireland Census Returns
Official Government Census Returns taken on the 31st March 1901 are available on line free of charge at www.nationalarchives. ie and on microfilm at NAI and WL; also on microfilm at the LDS

1901 census return for the McCormack family in Goldsmith Terrace, Athlone - see page 52.

Family History Library. The documents available are; Form A (the household return) gives the name, age, religion, occupation, ability to read and write, marital status, relationship to head of household, county of birth (or, if born outside of Ireland, the country), ability to speak English or Irish and whether suffering from certain disabilities. The age is questionable as older people may not have known their exact age and many were illiterate. It is always worth comparing ages stated in 1901 and 1911 census returns. - see page 53

Form BI lists the number of rooms occupied, the number of windows in the front of the house and the type of roof thereby allowing one to visualise the home of ones ancestors.

1908 - 1922 Census Search Forms

The Pension Act of 1908 provided an income to those who had attained 70 years of age and were of limited means. As a result verification of age became an issue. As civil records commenced only in 1864, birth certificates were not available and many parishes did not have baptismal records pre-1838. Therefore searches were made in the 1841 and 1851 census returns by the Public Record Office of Ireland (NAI) to provide applicants with proof of age. The application forms were called Census Search Forms or 'green forms' and they provide the details submitted by the applicant and the certified result of the search. They may be accessed at the NAI Ref.: MFGS59/ 1-27 or on-line (for a fee) at www.irelandgenealogy.com. This contains 221 entries for Westmeath.

Preceded by a search index the forms give the full name of the applicant, address, full names of father and mother of applicant, name of head of family (if other than father) with which the applicant resided in 1841 or 1851, relationship and occupation, residence in 1841 or 1851, county, barony, parish, townland, and street (if in a town). Unsuccessful searches are marked by an 'X' in the index. Additional names of other family members are entered on some of the forms.

1911 Government of Ireland Census Returns

The official government census returns taken on 2nd April 1911 provides more information than in 1901 (see page 55). Married women were required to include how many years their present

CENSUS OF IRELAND, 1911.

Two Examples of the mode of filling up this Table are given on the other side.

FORM A.

No. on Form B.

RETURN of the MEMBERS of this FAMILY and their VISITORS, BOARDERS, SERVANTS, &c., who slept or abode in this House on the night of SUNDAY, the 2nd of APRIL, 1911.

Christian Names	Surname	RELATION to Head of Family	RELIGIOUS PROFESSION	EDUCATION	Age (Males)	Age (Females)	RANK, PROFESSION, OR OCCUPATION	PARTICULARS AS TO MARRIAGE	WHERE BORN	IRISH LANGUAGE
Michael	Curran	Head	Roman Catholic	Read+write	53	–	Herd	Married	Co. Westmeath	–
Lizzie	Curran	Wife	R. Catholic	Read+write	–	43		Married 26 7 6	Co. Westmeath	–
Mary	Curran	Daughter	R. Catholic	Read+write	–	24		Single	Co. Westmeath	–
Patrick	Curran	Son	R. Catholic	Read+write	18	–	Agricultural Labourer	Single	Co. Westmeath	–
Jane	Curran	Daughter	R. Catholic	Read+write	–	13	Scholar	Single	Co. Westmeath	–
Matthew	Curran	Son	R. Catholic	Read+write	10	–	Scholar	Single	Co. Westmeath	–
Agnes	Curran	Daughter	R. Catholic	Read+write	–	9	Scholar	Single	Co. Westmeath	–

I hereby certify, as required by the Act 10 Edw. VII., and 1 Geo. V., cap. 11, that the foregoing Return is correct, according to the best of my knowledge and belief.

Francis Gallaugher, Signature of Enumerator.

I believe the foregoing to be a true Return.

Michael Curran, Signature of Head of Family.

1911 census return for the Curran family in the townland of Ballagh in Mullingar - see page opposite.

marriage had lasted, how many children were born alive in the present marriage and how many of them were still alive. Available on line and free of charge at www.nationalarchives.ie where copies of the original returns can also be downloaded in pdf format. It is also available on microfilm at the NAI and WL. (See also 1901)

General and Miscellaneous Sources

1593-1860 Alumni Dublinenses

A 'Register of the Students, Graduates, Professors and Provosts of Trinity College, in the University of Dublin from 1593 -1860'. Gives details of dates of admission, fathers name and occupation, subject and date of degrees (where relevant) etc. Compiled by G.D.Burtchaell (q.v.) and T.U. Sadlier and published by Thom's Dublin 1935. The publication covering the period 1593-1860 is available in the NLI. Also a CD covering the period up to 1846 is available from www.archivecdbooks.ie and can also be found on-line at www.findmypast.ie See below.

MALLORY, THOMAS, Pen. (Mr Carr, Dublin), May 16, 1657, aged 16 more or less ; s. of George, Minister ; b. Castle Jordan, Co. Westmeath.   Sch. and B.A. 1660.

MALONE, ANTHONY, S.C. (Mr Young, Dublin), Nov. 7, 1717, aged 16 ; s. of Richard, Jurisperitus ; b. Grangemore, Co. Westmeath.   LL.D. (honoris causa) Æst. 1737.   [Irish Bar 1726 ; P.C. ; Chancellor of the Exchequer (I.).] See *Foster* and *D. N. B.*

MALONE, ANTHONY, Pen. (Dr Garnett), June 2, 1735, aged 17 ; s. of Richard, Armiger ; b. Co. Westmeath.   B.A. Vern. 1739.   M.A. Vern. 1754.

Typical entries from the *Alumni Dublinenses*

1695-1905. Moran Manuscripts

Malachy J. Moran published material of local interest in the Westmeath Independent. His major work 'Records of Athlone and district' contains local information (1695-1905). They are available on microfilm at NLI Mss. 1543-1547; SLC film 0100214-216 and WL

1800-1899. Grand Jury Abstract of Presentments Books

These books detail public works contracts for 1800-1899. WL also SLC film 1279283). For example: *215. to John Lyons, esq., Peter Keeffe, and James Fay, to repair 65 perches, 16 feet wide, with small stones and gravel, road from Mullingar to Athlone, between James Murray's, of Cabbage-street, And the Widow Reddy's in Grange, 15 2s. 6d. per...*

1849-1921 Board of Guardians' Minute Books

These are the administration records of the poor law system which occasionally record mames of individuals. Records for Athlone Union (1849-1920) and Mullingar Union (1857-1921) are held in WL. No records survive for Delvin Union.

1914-1918 First World War Memorial Records

Memorial records of 49,400 Irishmen in the British Army (and some for other services) who died in the Great War. A memorial list was publishd in 1923 by the Irish National War Memorials Commission. The entries provide: Name; Regiment number; Rank; Place and Date of death; and (usually) place of birth. A fully searchable CD with images of every page is available from Eneclann at www.eneclann.ie (see below).

CURLEY, MICHAEL. Reg. No. 7261. Rank, Sergeant, Connaught Rangers, 6th Batt. ; died of wounds, France, August 3, 1917 ; born St. Mary's, Athlone, Co. Westmeath.

A typical entry from the *First World War Memorials* - see above

Argentine Records

Many Westmeath people emigrated to Argentina and the link is kept alive by the Longford Westmeath Argentina Society which may be contacted at longfordwestmeathargentinasoc@yahoo.com. Useful sources include:

Eduardo Coghlan, *Los Irlandeses En La Argentina, Buenos Aires*, 1987 is an account of the Irish immigrants (written in Spanish). It can be consulted at WL. *The Southern Cross*, organ of Irish and Catholic interests in the River Plate (Newspaper founded 1875) is available on microfilm at the NLI and WL. Edmundo Murray, *Becoming Irlandés; Private Narratives of the Irish Emigration to Argentina (1844-1912)*, Bunenos Aires, 2006.
A list of passengers to Argentina may be viewed at www.irlandeses. org/passenger.htm

Burgess Papers

(Papers relating to Athlone c1571-1881, 26 vols.) Dr. John Buchanan Burgess was a noted local historian born in 1885. His collection includes; Directories: deeds: newspapers: biographies: vestry minutes of St. Mary's Church 1750-1888; register of Kiltoom and Camma (baptisms c.1797-c.1943), marriages 1802-1910 and burials 1801-1943); register of St. Mary, Athlone (1747-1849); Willbrook Church, Methodist (Athlone) and Drumraney Churches: St. Peter's c.1845-c.1870, Kilkenny West 1783-1862; Bunowen burials 1824-1941. Available on microfilm at NLI P.5309; SLC 1279272 and WL. For a full description see N.W. English, The Burgess Papers of Athlone, in J. Old Athlone Society, 1, (4), 1974-75, pp. 254-262 and 2, (5), 1978, pp. 71-74.

Photograph Collections:

National Photographic Archive www.nli.ie. The Irish Architectural Archive www.archeire.com/iaa. WL holds a limited collection. See also *Photographs and photography in Irish local History* by Liam Kelly, Dublin, Four Courts Press, 2008.

1791 - 1853 Transportation Records

Records of convicts transported to Australia (1788 and 1868) are available online at www.nationalarchives.ie and on microfilm at the NAI. A useful source is, Micheál Ó Conláin, *The Westmeath Transportation Lists;* compiled from archive and newspaper reports, Castlepollard, 2006, (typescript) WL.

Chapter 6   Church Records

Church records are usually the earliest and most comprehensive source available to those who seek their ancestors. The Census of Ireland 1861 records that out of a total population of 90,879 in Westmeath, 83,749 (92%) were Roman Catholics, 6,336 (7%) Church of Ireland (CoI), 343 Presbyterians, 156 Methodists, 73 Baptists, 51 Society of Friends or Quakers, 2 Independents and 169 all other persuasions. In short, 99% were either Catholic or Church of Ireland. The various religious denominations have their own parish structures and their own practices for recording baptisms, marriages and (sometimes) deaths/burials. The availability and quality of records varies greatly between these different denominations for a wide variety of reasons. *Irish Church Records* by James G. Ryan (Flyleaf Press 2001) provides a comprehensive account of the records maintained by eight denominations, including the history of their compilation, the types of records available and where they are currently available.

Below is a brief background to the religious denominations in Westmeath.

Catholic Church Parish Records

The nature and availability of Catholic records has been greatly affected by the course of Irish history. Although it was the church of the vast majority, the Roman Catholic Church was effectively a proscribed organization from the Banishment Act of 1697 until the Catholic Relief Act of 1782 and this precarious status, even though the Penal Laws were not always rigorously enforced, affected record-keeping.

TABLE 5.2

Abbreviations and Terms Commonly Used in Catholic Church Records

Bapt.	*Baptised*
conj.	*"conjunxi": ie joined in marriage*
coram	*in the presence of*
cum dispens-atione in bannis	*With dispensation by Banns. (see p.126)*
Derelictus	*Abandoned i.e abandoned child*
de.	*"of" usually denoting a person as being "of " a particular place or a child as being "of " a parent*
Dau.	*daughter*
et	*and*
Filia	*daughter of (parent's name)*
Filius	*son of (parent's name)*
fil.leg.	*"Filius;/Filia legitimus/a"Legitimate son/daughter*
ignotes parentibus	*parents unknown*
Gemini	*Twins*
Illeg	*Illegitimate*
in tertio/ quattuor etc consanguineo	*Where the bride or groom were closely related, dispensation was needed to allow them to marry. The degree of relationship was stated in the dispensation, eg "tertio consanguineo" means that the couple were first cousins; "quattor consanguineo" that they were second cousins etc.*
Patrini	*A term occasionally used for Sponsors*
Peregrini	*Travellers*
Sp.	*"Sponsoribus" ie the Sponsors or Godparents*
Ss. or Sps.	*Sponsors i.e Godparents*
Sub Conditione	*A child considered to be in danger of death, or apparently dead, could be baptised by the mother or other person. This child was subsequently also baptised by the priest "sub conditione" or "on condition" that the earlier emergency administration of the baptism had not been performed correctly. This annotation suggests that the child was in poor health at birth but had survived.*
Test.	*"Testibus;" or Testator ie Witness*
Ws.	*Witness(es) (in the case of a marriage)*

A table of Latin terms used in Catholic Church Records from
'Irish Church Records'
Ed. by James G. Ryan (Flyleaf Press 2001)
This publication provides a history and description of records kept
by the Quaker, Church of Ireland, Presbyterian, Catholic, Methodist,
Jewish, Huguenot and Baptist denominations in Ireland.

The Penal Laws, enacted during the late 17th and early 18th centuries, after the defeat of the Jacobite cause, deprived Catholics of their rights and employment opportunities. One affect was that Catholic Churches in many areas had few resources and priests, and record-keeping suffered. Nevertheless, there are excellent records in certain areas – but most parish records in Westmeath (and other counties) date from the nineteenth century. The original records are held in their individual parishes, but copies of these up to 1880 and in some cases up to 1900 are held on microfilm in the NLI (indexed under diocese). A catalogue of the RC registers is available on line at www.nli.ie. In addition, the Dún na Sí Heritage Centre (see page 153) have indexed church records for Westmeath. These may be searched on line at www.rootsireland.ie A name search brings up relevant entries and more details for a particular name may be viewed for a fee.

Westmeath parishes are mainly in the Diocese of Meath, with some, in the West of the county, in the Diocese of Ardagh and Clonmacnoise. Some parish priests will allow access to the records, others to the index only and some will conduct a search themselves. Contact details for Catholic parishes in the diocese of Meath can be found online at www.dioceseofmeath.ie and for Ardagh and Clonmacnois at www. ardaghdiocese.org. Contact details for Catholic parishes are also to be found listed alphabetically in the Irish Catholic Directory which is published annually.

Time and patience may be required to decipher the original records as they are very variable in style and state of preservation. Many are recorded in Latin.

In the case of baptisms the record usually includes date, name of child, name of father, mother's maiden name and the name of sponsors. Children were normally baptised within a few days of birth where this was geographically possible, and where the child was able to travel. It is fair to assume that the date of baptism is fairly close to the date of birth. For marriages the records typically include date, names of those marrying and names of witnesses. The place of residence is sometimes given. Marriages normally took place in the bride's parish, but a search of adjoining parishes may prove fruitful. Death records are uncommon and where they exist generally only give the person's name and date of death; occasionally an address will be provided.

The following list shows, for each civil parish, the Catholic Parish(es) which served the area; the dates for which records are available and where they may be obtained (e.g. in the National Library (NLI), and Dun Na Sí (i.e. they are indexed by the local Heritage centre – see page 153.

Civil Parish: Ardnurcher or Horseleap
Map Grid: 50
Catholic Parish: Clara (Kilbride 1 Co. Offaly and Horseleap,
            Co. Westmeath.
Diocese: ME
Bapt: 2.1845-12.1880 NLI P.4174: 1845-1899 (includes Clara) Dún na Sí
Marr: 11.1821-11.1880 NLI P.4174: 1821-1899 (includes Clara) Dún na Sí
Death: 1.1825-2.1854; 10.1864-10.1868 NLI P.4174: 1825-1868
(missing 1826, 1832-1835, 1855-1863) (includes Clara) Dún na Sí

Civil Parish: Ballyloughloe
Map Grid: 46
Catholic Parish: Ballyloughloe; (Mount Temple, Moate and Kilcleagh)
see Kilcleagh (1)
Diocese: ME
Bapt: 1816- -1899, (missing 1818-1824) Dún na Sí
Marr: 1824-1899 (missing 1852) Dún na Sí
Death: 1824-1899 (missing 1826-1833) Dún na Sí

Civil Parish: Ballymore
Map Grid: 36
Catholic Parish: Ballymore
Diocese: ME
Bapt: 9.1824-9.1841; 3.1839-12.1880 NLI P.4171; 1824-1899 Dún na Sí
Marr: 4.1839-9.1870; 2.1872-11.1880 NLI P.4171: 1839-1899 (missing
1870-1871) Dún na Sí

Civil Parish: Ballymorin
Map Grid: 38
Catholic Parish: Milltown, see Rathconrath

Civil Parish: Bunown/Benown
Map Grid 30
Catholic Parish: see Drumraney

Civil Parish: Carrick
Map Grid; 59
Catholic Parish: part Rochfortbridge, see Castlelost; part Mullingar

Civil Parish: Castlelost
Map Grid: 63
Catholic Parish: Rochfortbridge
Diocese: ME
Bapt: 6.1823-12.1856; 1.1857-12.1880 NLI P.4172: 1822-1900 Dún na Sí
Marr 12.1816-11.1880 NLI P.4172; 1817-1900 Dún na Sí

Civil Parish: Castletownkindalen
Map Grid: 51
Catholic Parish: Castletown-Geoghegan
Diocese: ME
Bapt: 8.1829-3.1850; 3.1846-12.1880; 6.1861-12.1880 (separate registers cover same dates) NLI P.4169; 1829-1900 Dún na Sí
Marr: 2.1829-3.1835; 7.1835-2.1850 (few entries 1846-1850); 10.1846-5.1880; 1.1862-11.1880 (separate registers for same dates) NLI P.4169; 1829-1900 Dún na Sí
Death; 4.1829-4.1835 NLI P.4169: 1829-1844 (missing 1834, 1836, 1840) Dún na Sí

Civil Parish: Churchtown
Map Grid; 40
Catholic Parish: Dysart or Churchtown
Diocese: ME
Bapt: 8.1836-8.1862; 4.1861-12.1880 NLI P.4168: 1836-1899 Dún na Sí
Marr: 2.1825-2.1862: 1825-1899 Dún na Sí

Civil Parish: Clonarney
Map Grid; 24
Catholic Parish: Clonmellon, see Killua

Civil Parish: Clonfad
Map Grid; 62
Catholic Parish: Rochfortbridge, see Castlelost

Civil Parish: Conry
Map Grid: 39
Catholic Parish: see Churchtown

Civil Parish: Delvin
Map Grid 39
Catholic Parish: Delvin or Castletowndelvin
Bapt: 1.1785-3.1789; 7.1792-7.1812; 7.1830-12.1880 NLI P.4172: 1785-1900 (missing 1790, 1791, 1813-1830) Dún na Sí
Marr: 2.1785-3.1789; 7.1792-7.1812; 9.1830-10.1880 NLI P.4172: 1785-1900 (missing 1790-1791, 1794, 1813-1829) Dún na Sí
Death: 2.1785-3.1789; 7.1792-7.1812; 1.1849-4.1855 NLI P.4172: 1785-1855 (missing 1790, 1791, 1813-1848) Dún na Sí

Civil Parish: Drumraney
Map Grid; 32
Catholic Parish: Drumraney (Noughaval)
Diocese: ME
Bapt: 4.1834-12.1880 NLI P.4171: 1834-1900 Dún na Sí
Marr; 5.1834-9.1880 NLI P.4171: 1834-1898 (missing 1853, 1896) Dún na Sí
Death: 1819-1820

Civil Parish: Durrow (Co. Offaly)
Map Grid; 54
Catholic Parish: Durrow (Westmeath and Offaly)
Diocese: ME
(Durrow contains all or part of the following Westmeath townlands: Ballybroder, Ballycahan, Cappalahy, Derrygolan, Frevanagh, Keeloge, Pallas and Rostalla)
Bapt: 3.1836-12.1880 NLI P.4174
Marr; 1809 and 1810 (a few at end) NLI P.4174

Civil Parish: Dysart
Map Grid: 43
Catholic Parish: see Churchtown

Civil Parish: Enniscoffey
Map Grid; 58
Catholic Parish: Rochfortbridge,see Castlelost

Civil Parish: Faughalstown
Map Grid: 7
Catholic Parish: Turbotstown, see Mayne

Civil Parish: Foyran
Map Grid: 1
Catholic Parish: Castlepollard, see Rathgarve

Civil Parish: Kilbeggan
Map Grid: 52
Catholic Parish: Kilbeggan
Bapt; 11.1818-8.1824; 4.1825-12.1859; 1.1860-12.1880 NLI P.4176; 1818-1900 Dún na Sí
Marr: 10.1818-11.1859; 1.1860-11.1880 NLI P.4176; 1818-1900 Dún na Sí
Death: 9.1818-12.1843 NLI P.4176: 1818-1884 (missing 1844-1862, 1880, 1881, 1883) Dún na Sí

Civil Parish: Kilbixy
Map Grid: 13
Catholic Parish: Sonna and Ballinacarrigy
Diocese: ME
Bapt: 9.1837-12.1880 NLI P.4168: 1837-1892 Dún na Sí
Marr: 11.1838-7.1880 NLI P.4168; 1839-1899 (missing 1843, 1882) Dún na Sí

Civil Parish: Kilbride
Map Grid 60
Catholic Parish: Rochfortbridge. See Castlelost

Civil Parish: Kilcleagh (1)
Map Grid: 47
Catholic Parish: Kilcleagh (Moate and Mount Temple) See Ballyloughloe

Civil Parish: Kilcleagh (2)
Map Grid: 47
Catholic Parish: Lemanaghan or Balnahowen/Ballinahown (Westmeath and Offaly).
Diocese: AC
Bapt; 8.1821-12.1824; 2.1826-2.1839; 2.1841-9.1845; 7.1854-12.1880 NLI P.4235; 1830-1899 Dún na Sí
Marr: 1.1830-8.1845; 10.1854-11.1880 NLI P.4235; 1830-1899 Dún na Sí
Death: 11.1829-9.1845; 9.1854-12.1880 NLI P.4235: 1830-1899 Dún na Sí

Civil Parish: Kilcumny
Map Grid: 23
Catholic Parish: Collinstown; see St. Feighin's

Civil Parish: Kilcumreragh
Map Grid: 49
Catholic Parish: Tubber (includes Rosemount)
Diocese: ME
Bapt: 11.1821-12.1880 NLI P.4176; 1820-1899 (missing 1822) Dún na Sí
Marr: 11.1824-12.1880 NLI P.4176; 1824-1899 Dún na Sí
Death: 1824-1872 (missing 1843-1844, 1847-1849, 1851-1854, 1863, 1866-1869) Dún na Sí

Civil Parish: Kilkenny West
Map Grid: 49
Catholic Parish: Tubberclair (Glasson)
Diocese: ME
Bapt: 8.1829-12.1880 NLI P.4171; 1829-1899 (missing 1845-1846) Dún na Sí
Marr:1829-1899 (missing 1846) Dún na Sí

Civil Parish: Killagh
Map Grid: 28
Catholic Parish: see Delvin

Civil Parish: Killare
Map Grid; 37
Catholic Parish: see Ballymore

Civil Parish: Killua
Map Grid: 25
Catholic Parish: Clonmellon
Diocese: ME
Bapt: 1.1759-9.1784; 2.1785-3.1809; 6.1819-8.1872 NLI P.4187; 1759-1900 (missing 1777-1778, 1810-1814, 1816-1818) Dún na Sí
Marr: 1.1757-9.1809; 1.1815-2.1815; 7.1819-7.1845; 1.1846-6.1872. NLI P.4187; 1757-1900 (missing 1772-1773, 1777-1779, 1783, 1810-1814, 1816-1818, 1871) Dún na Sí
Death: 1.1757-10.1809; 11.1819-7.1850 NLI P.4187: 1757-1850, missing 1771, 1773, 1779, 1783, 1786, 1810-1819, Dún na Sí

Civil Parish: Killucan (1)
Map Grid; 44
Catholic Parish: Killucan (Raharney and Rathwire)
Diocese: ME
Bapt: 7.1838-1.1875; 1.1875-12.1880 NLI P.4166: 1821-1899 Dún na Sí
Marr: 5.1821-11.1880 NLI P.4166: 1821-1899 Dún na Sí
(Raharney and Rathwire (Killucan) Bapt 5.1821-7.1838 NLI P.4166

Civil Parish: Killucan (2)
Map Grid: 44
Catholic Parish: Kinnegad
Diocese: ME
Bapt: 6.1827-12.1880 NLI P.4170: 1827-1899 (missing 1839) Dún na Sí
Marr: 7.1844-9.1880 NLI P.4170: 1842-1900 Dún na Sí
Death: 1869-1884 Dún na Sí

Civil Parish: Killulagh
Map Grid: 26
Catholic Parish: see Delvin

Civil Parish: Kilmacnevan
Map Grid 12
Catholic Parish: see Rathconrath

Civil parish: Kilmanaghan (Westmeath and Offaly)
Map Grid: 48
Catholic Parish: Moate, see Kilcleagh 1

Civil Parish: Kilpatrick
Map Grid: 8
Catholic Parish: Collinstown, see St. Feighin's

Civil Parish: Lackan
Map Grid: 15
Catholic Parish: see Multyfarnham

Civil Parish: Leney
Map Grid: 17
Catholic Parish: see Multyfarnham

Civil Parish: Lickblea
Map Grid: 2
Catholic Parish: Castlepollard, includes Lickblea and Wheran, Rathgarraf (see Rathgarve).
Diocese: ME
Bapt; 1.1763-3.1765; 10.1771-6.1790 NLI P.4164
Marr; 1763-6.1790 NLI P.4164
Death: 3.1764-6.1790 NLI P.4164

Civil Parish: Lynn
Map Grid; 56
Catholic Parish: see Mullingar

Civil Parish: Mayne
Map Grid: 3
Catholic Parish: Turbotstown, Coole, or Mayne
Diocese: ME
Bapt; 8.1777-5.1796; 1.1798-11.1820; 4.1824-4.1835; 2.1847-8.1863 (missing pages) NLI P.4167: 1777-1899 (missing 1801, 1821-1823, 1836-1846, 1851-1852) Dún na Sí
Marr: 11.1777-4.1796; 1.1798-12.1820; 5.1824-7.1843; 4.1846-7.1863; 11.1864-7.1880 NLI P.4167; 1778-1899 (missing 1793, 1821-1823, 1844-1863, Dún na Sí
Death; 8.1777-11.1796; 2.1803-9.1820; 4.1824-8.1844; 1.1846-7.1850; 1.1864-10.1869; NLI P.4167: 1777-1869 (missing 1791-1793, 1799-1802, 1819, 1821-1823, 1845-1863) Dún na Sí

Civil Parish: Moylisker
Map Grid; 57
Catholic Parish: see Mullingar

Civil Parish: Mullingar
Map Grid: 42
Catholic Parish: Mullingar
Diocese: ME
Bapt; fragment 1741-42; 7.1742-7.1785 NLI P.4161; 7.1785-5.1800; 1.1800-4.1816; 5.1825-12.1832; NLI P.4162; 1.1833-11.1842; 11.1843-12.1880 NLI P.4163; Index to Baptisms Vol. D-K 1741-1816 P9486; Index to Baptisms Vol. L-R 1825-1900 P9487; 1742-1900 (with gaps) indexed WL; 1737-1900 (missing 1747, 1820, -1822) Dún na Sí

Marr; 10.1737-7.1754; 7.1792-11.1812 NLI P.4161; 1.1779-7.1792; 11.1812-4.1824; NLI P.4162; 1.1833-4.1859; 5.1860-11.1880 NLI P.4163: 1737-1900 (with gaps) indexed WL; 1737-1900 (missing 1824-1833) Dún na Sí
Death; 5.1757-10.1797 NLI P.4161; 1.1833-5.1838; 2.1843-1880 NLI P.4163:

Civil Parish: Multyfarnham
Map Grid; 16
Catholic Parish: Multyfarnham
Diocese: ME
Bapt; 2.1824-12.1880 NLI P.4168; 1824-1899 Dún na Sí
Marr; 2.1824-6.1880 NLI P.4168; 1824-1899 (missing 1881, 1890) Dún na Sí
Death; 1.1831-7.1844 NLI P.4168; 1831-1848 (missing 1845,1847) Dún na Sí

Civil Parish: Newtown
Map Grid: 53
Catholic Parish: see Castletownkindalen

Civil Parish: Noughaval
Map Grid: 29
Catholic Parish: Tang, see also Drumraney for earlier records
Diocese: ME
Bapt: 1857-1899 (missing 1892) Dún na Sí
Marr: 1858-1899 (missing 1887-1888;1892,1893) Dún na Sí

Civil Parish: Pass of Kilbride
Map Grid: 61
Catholic Parish: Rochfortbridge, see Castlelost

Civil Parish: Piercetown
Map Grid: 33
Catholic Parish: Moyvore, see Templepatrick

Civil Parish: Portloman
Map Grid: 22
Catholic Parish: see Mullingar

Civil Parish: Portnashangan
Map Grid; 19
Catholic Parish: see Multyfarnham

Civil Parish: Rahugh
Map Grid; 55
Catholic Parish: see Kilbeggan

Civil Parish: Rathaspick
Map Grid: 11
Catholic Parish: Rathowen (Rathaspick and Russagh)
Diocese; AC
Bapt; 3.1822-9.1826; 7.17.1821-4.1833; 5.1836-10.1846; 3.1847-12.1880
NLI P.4236: 1822-1900 (missing 1827, 1829-1831, 1833-1835) Dún na Sí
Marr; 12.1819-2.1826; 10.1832-10.1833; 1.1838-11.1843; 1.1844-11.1880
NLI P.4236; 1821-1899 (missing 1827-1831, 1834-1837, 1896) Dún na Sí
Death: 3.1822-2.1826; 8.1832-11.1833; 8.1837-10.1843; 2.1844-12.1880
NLI P.4236; 1815-1899 (missing 1816,1818, 1827, 1829-1831, 1834, 1836, 1884, 1896) Dún na Sí

Civil Parish: Rathconnell
Map Grid: 41
Catholic Parish: part Taghmon; part Mullingar

Civil Parish: Rathconrath
Map Grid: 34
Catholic Parish: Milltown
Diocese: ME
Bapt: 1.1781-9.1808; 4.1809-10.1825; 3.1826-11.1849; 2.1850-10.1869; 9.1869-12.1880 NLI P.4167; 1781-1900 (missing 1790) Dún na Sí
Marr; 1.1781-2.1805; 4.1809-10.1825; 3.1826-11.1849; 2.1850-10.1869; 11.1869-10.1880 NLI P.4167; 1781-1900 (missing 1790, 1806-1808) Dún na Sí
Death; 1.1781-11.1808; 4.1809-10.1825; 3.1826-11.1849; 2.1850-10.1869
NLI P4167: 1781-1872 (missing1782,1790, 1871, 1873-1874, 1876-1881) Dún na Sí

Civil Parish: Rathgarve
Map Grid: 4
Catholic Parish: Castlepollard
Diocese: ME
Bapt: 1.1795-8.1805; 8.1805-3.1837 NLI P.4164; 3.1837-12.1880 NLI P.4165
Marr: 3.1793-8.1793; 1.1795-6.1825 NLI P.4164; 11.1825-9.1875 NLI P.4165
Death: 1.1793-6.1825 NLI P.4614
(See also Lickblea)

Civil Parish: Russagh
Map Grid: 10
Catholic Parish: see Rathaspick

Civil Parish: St. Feighin's
Map Grid: 5
Catholic Parish: Collinstown (Fore)
Diocese: ME
Bapt: 2.1807-4.1815; 3.1821-11.1843; 3.1844-12.1880 NLI P.4169
Marr; 6.1784-11.1880 NLI P.4169

Civil Parish: St. Mary's
Map Grid: 6
Catholic Parish: Collinstown, see St. Feighin's

Civil Parish: St. Mary's Athlone
Map Grid: 45
Catholic Parish: St. Mary's Athlone
Diocese: AC
Bapt: 1.1813-9.1826; 2.1827-3.1827; 5.1839-4.1852; 2.1853-2.1868 NLI
P.4242; 1813-1891 (missing 1821, 1828-1832, 1836, 1859-61) Dún na Sí
Marr: 1.1813-4.1827; 1.1834-12.1851; 2.1854-2.1863 NLI P.4242; 1813-
1899 (missing 1828, 1830, 1832-1833, 1867) Dún na Sí.
Death: 1.1813-9.1826; 2.1827-3.1827; 6.1819-12.1826 NLI P.4242;
1813-1826 Dún na Sí

Civil Parish: St. Peter's Athlone (Westmeath and Roscommon)
Catholic Parish: St. Peter's Athlone and Drum (Westmeath and
Roscommon)
Diocese: EL
Bapt: 1.1789-12.1880 NLI P.4615
Marr: 1.1789-9.1864 NLI P.4615
Death: 1.1789-10.1880 NLI P.4615

Civil Parish: Stonehall
Map Grid: 18
Catholic Parish: see Taghmon

Civil Parish: Street
Map Grid: 9
Catholic Parish: Street
Diocese: AC
Bapt: 7.1820-7.1827; 11.1831-12.1831; 12.1834-12.1880 NLI P.4236; 1820-1900 (missing 1832-1837) Dún na Sí
Marr: 8.1820-1.1.1828; 1.1835-1.1.1841 NLI P.4236: 1820-1900 (missing 1825-1848, 1857-1886) Dún na Sí
Death: 9.1823-8.1829; 12.1834-1.1841; 7.1842-12.1880 NLI P.4236; 1724-1899 (missing 1884,1885)) Dún na Sí

Civil Parish: Taghmon
Map Grid: 21
Catholic Parish: Taghmon
Diocese: ME
Bapt: 9.1781-3.1790; 3.1809-12.1840; 1.1841-12.1850; 1.1864-12.1880 NLI P.4165; 1781-1886 (missing 1791-99, 1801-08, 1851-53, 1855-56, 1859-62) Dún na Sí
Marr: 1.1782-7.1791; 8.1809-5.1848; 9.1863-11.1880 NLI P.4165; 1782-1848 (missing 1792-1799, 1801-08) Dún na Sí
Death: 9.1809-2.1848 NLI P.4165; 1809-1868 Dún na Sí

Civil Parish: Templeoran
Map Grid; 14
Catholic Parish: Sonna, see Kilbixy

Civil Parish: Templepatrick or Moyvore
Map Grid: 35
Catholic Parish: Moyvore
Diocese: ME
Bapt; 9.1831-12.1880 NLI P.4171: 1831-1899 Dún na Sí
Marr; 2.1832-11.1880 NLI P.4171; 1831-1899 (missing 1850) Dún na Sí
Death; 3.1831-9.1865 (missing 4.1852-5.1863) NLI P.4171; 1831-1872 (missing 1839-1841, 1853-1861, 1866-1872) Dún na Sí

Civil Parish: Tyfarnham
Map Grid; 20
Catholic Parish: see Taghmon

Church of Ireland Parish Records

During the 16th century the Church of Ireland was established, and the State took over the Catholic Church infrastructure and its institutions. However, large parts of Ireland were not within the control of the English administration, and the vast majority of the population was not amenable to the change. The old administrative divisions were adopted and used as territorial divisions by the new church, but the boundaries and practices gradually changed over the centuries. It is very important to note the significance of the Church of Ireland as the State or Established Church. Until 1858, the state maintained a Church as part of its administration. Its duties included probate (see page 95). licensing of marriages and other minor roles. It also had the power to fund its activities from a tax (see Tithes page 82) which was payable by all citizens. Its records also had a legal status and were admissible as evidence of marriage, birth, etc. A full account of the history and nature of Church of Ireland records is given by Raymond Refausse in a chapter of *Irish Church Records* (Flyleaf Press, 2001).

The Parochial Records (Ireland) Act 1875 specified that Church of Ireland marriage records pre-1845 and birth and burial records pre-1871 were public records and should be moved for safe-keeping to the Public Record Office in Dublin. This requirement was, fortunately, resisted by many parishes; while others kept copies of the records which they had transmitted to Dublin. By 1922, more than 60% of C of I Parish records had been deposited in the PRO and almost all of these were destroyed in a fire in 1922. However, taking the original records not deposited and the copies made prior to deposit, about 60% of the pre-1871 records have survived. Today some Church of Ireland records are held in the NAI, some in the Representative Church Body Library (RCBL) and others remain in local custody. See also www.rootsireland.ie.

Church of Ireland parishes in Westmeath are within the Church of Ireland Diocese of Meath and Kildare and are incorporated into three divisions namely Athlone, Castlepollard (Rathgraffe) and Mullingar. Churches in the Athlone division include Athlone, St. Mary, Benown, St. Canice, Clonmacnoise, St. Kieran, Forgney, St. Munis, Moate, St. Mary; Castlepollard includes Drumcree, St. John, Kilbride Castlecor Oldcastle, St. Bride: Mullingar includes Almoritia, St. Nicholas, Kilbixey, St. Bigseach, Killucan, St. Etchen, Mullingar, All Saints. It is important to remember that Catholics were often buried in Church of Ireland burial places and therefore would have been listed in their burial registers.

The following is a list of records and their access (The name of the Civil Parish is included only when it differs from the CoI Parish name):
CoI Parish: Ardnurcher or Horseleap
Bapt: 1873-1982 RCBL; 1871-1900 Dún na Sí
Marr: 1848-1974 RCBL; 1819-76 NAI MFCI 62; 1846-1892 Dún na Sí
Death: 1882-1899 Dún na Sí

CoI Parish: Ballyloughloe
Bapt: 1877-1955 RCBL; 1877-1899 Dún na Sí
Marr: 1845-1945 RCBL: 1845-1897 Dún na Sí
Burl: 1877-1970 RCBL; 1882-1899 Dún na Sí

CoI Parish: Ballymore
Bapt: 1878-1937 RCBL
Marr: 1850-1923 RCBL
Burl: 1878-1985 RCBL; 1700-1900 Dún na Sí

Civil Parish: Ballymorin
CoI Parish: Almoritia
Marr: 1846-1937 RCBL
Burl: 1800-1900 Dún na Sí

CoI Parish: Bunown or Benown
Bapt: 1819-1999 RCBL (incomplete); 1819-1876 NAI MFCI 61; 1809-1861 Dún na Sí
Marr: 1847-1934 RCBL (incomplete);
Burl: 1824-1999 RCBL (incomplete); 1824-1941 NLI Pos. 5309; 1829-1877 NAI MFCI 61; 1824-1941 SLC film 1279272; 1833-1897 Dún na Sí: 1824-1941 BP
Vestry Minutes: 1820-1879, with index to persons SLC film 1279272:

CoI Parish: Carrick, see Moylisker

CoI Parish: Castlelost
Bapt: 1883-1971 RCBL
Marr: 1850-1980 RCBL
Burl: 1882-1987 RCBL

CoI Parish: Castletownkindalen or Vastina
Bapt: 1850-1939 RCBL; 1850-77 NAI MFCI 54
Marr: 1845-1938 RCBL
Burl: 1878-1962 RCBL
CoI Parish: Churchtown
Marr: 1846-1976 RCBL

CoI Parish: Clonfad (Clonfadforan)
Bapt: 1884-1997 RCBL
Marr: 1845-1954 RCBL
Burl: 1884-1993 RCBL

CoI Parish: Delvin
Bapt: 1817-1947 RCBL: NAI MFCI 51
Marr: 1817-1942 RCBL; 1817 – 1950 NAI MFCI 51
Burl: 1817-1989 RCBL; 1817-1943 NAI MFCI 51

CoI Parish: Drumraney
Marr: 1847-1866 Dún na Sí; BP
Burl: 1819 (4 records) 1820 Dún na Sí

CoI Parish: Enniscoffey
Bapt: 1881-1953 RCBL
Marr: 1845-1925 RCBL
Burl: 1891-1976 RCBL

CoI Parish: Foyran
Bapt: 1890-1960 RCBL
Marr: 1878-1939 RCBL

CoI Parish: Kilbeggan
Bapt: 1881-1959 RCBL
Marr: 1845-1940 RCBL
Burl: 1882-1988 RCBL

CoI Parish: Kilbixy
Bapt: 1824-1899 Dun na Sí HC
Marr: 1848-1947 RCBL; 1835-1837 Dun na Sí HC
Burl: 1821-1898 Dun na Sí HC

EXTRACTS FROM THE VESTRY BOOK AND PARISH REGISTERS OF KILBEGGAN, CO. WESTMEATH

contributed by the Rev. C. C. Ellison

The following extracts from the parish registers and vestry minutes of Kilbeggan were made by the Rev. William Reynell of 22, Eccles Street, Dublin, probably after the books had been deposited in the Public Record Office, where they were destroyed in 1922. It appears that there were three books: (1) Vestry Minutes, etc., with baptisms, marriages and burials from 1764 to 1826; (2) Register entries from 1822 to 1829; (3) Register entries from 1829 to 1880, containing 242 baptisms, 36 marriages and 104 burials.

The extracts are entered in pencil in a school exercise book, and evidently were made hurridly and almost at random. This exercise book, which also contains other jottings, is now Reynell Mss. No. 7 in the Meath Diocesan Registry.

Vestry Book Entries

No corpse to be buried in body of church under £1.

7 April 1765 (Church cess?) Shopkeeper, innkeeper, ale seller 1d. each. Shoemaker, wigmaker, butcher, clothier 6d each. Smith, tailor, cooper, hatter, huckster 3d each.

30 Sept. 1765. Herbert Bowen, minister, Wm Midgeley, Richard Rylands churchwardens. Gustavus Lambart, John Elrington, Francis Faulkner, Wm Fleetwood, Thomas Faulkner, Jonah Belton.

22 April 1783, Wm Midgeley signs. To 17 April 1781 Herbert Bowen signs as minister.

9 April 1787, Francis Taylor, minister. Pew on north side to J. W. Berry of Middleton to build a handsome new one.

21 April 1789. James Elrington, minister.

29 April 1791, Pew of Wm Midgeley Esq united to others.

7 April 1801, Wm Marshall, minister.

A page from the *Irish Ancestor*
Volume 9 (2) 1977, page 70 - 73, See above

CoI Parish: Kilcleagh
Bapt: 1873-1999 RCBL; 1829-1900 Dun na Sí HC
Marr: 1845-1956 RCBL; 1845-1899 Dun na Sí HC
Burl: 1876-1999 RCBL; 1792-1899 Dun na Sí HC

Civil Parish: Kilcumny
CoI Parish: Drumcree
Bapt: 1816-1983 RCBL; 1816-1875 NAI M5108/9; 1763-1862 SLC film 1279272
Marr: 1848-1977 RCBL; 1763-1862 SLC film 1279272
Burl: 1816-81 NAI M.5108-9; 1763-1862 SLC film 1279272
Vestry Minutes: 1795 1862 and 1861-1876, with index to persons SLC film 1279272

CoI Parish: Kilkenny West
Bapt: 1783-1956 RCBL 1783-1862 NLI P.5309; 1816-65 SLC film 990092; index SLC film 8838659; 1783-1876 Dun na Sí; 1783-1862 BP
Marr: 1783-1913 RCBL; 1783-1862 NLI P.5309; 1816-65 SLC film 990092: 1798-1855 Dun na Sí; 1783-1862 BP
Burl: 1784-1985 RCBL: 1783-1862 NLI P. 5309; 1809-1862 Dun na Sí; 1783-1862 BP
Confirmations: 1860-1867 BP
Vestry Minutes: 1795-1833-60-1876 NLI P.5309 BP

CoI Parish: Killucan
Bapt: 1696-1863 RCBL; 1696-1778 NLI p. 1997; 1696-1778 NLI GO 578; 1696-1778 RIA Upton Papers, No. 10; transcripts 1696-1795 and index SLC film 992663
Marr: 1787-1948 RCBL; 1788-1835 NLI p. 1997; ;1787-1855 RIA Upton Papers, No. 10; 1787-1929 SLC film 992663
Burl: 1700-1888 RCBL; 1700-1772 NLI p. 1997; 1700-72 NLI GO 578; 1700-1772 RIA Upton Papers, No. 10; 1700-72 and index SLC film 992663 also on SLC films 101011 and 100158
List of Church Wardens 1699-1800 RIA Upton Papers, no. 10.

CoI Parish: Kinnegad
Bapt: 1892-1917 RCBL
Marr: 1845-1894 RCBL
Burl: 1895-1956 RCBL

CoI Parish: Leney
Bapt: 1840-1977 RCBL; 1840-72 NAI MFCI 62; 1860-1899 Dún na Sí
Marr: 1845-1945 RCBL
Burl: 1840-1841 RCBL; 1860-71 NAI MFCI 62; 1860-1899 Dún na Sí

CoI Parish: Mayne
Bapt: 1808-1983 RCBL; 1808-70 NAI MFCI 51
Marr: 1809-1980 RCBL; 1809-70 NAI MFCI 51
Burl: 1808-1993 RCBL; 1808-70 NAI MFCI 51

CoI Parish: Moyliscar
Bapt: 1877-1989 RCBL
Marr: 1845-1990 RCBL; 1846-1899 SLC film 1279285; 1846-1899 WL (index)
Burl:1878-1988 RCBL; 1878-1900 SLC film 1279285; 1878-1900 WL (index)

CoI Parish: Mullingar
Bapt: 1849-1899 Dún na Sí; 1877-1900 WL (index)
Marr: 1845-1956 RCBL; 1739-1899 Dún na Sí ; SLC film 1279285;
1845-1900 WL (index)
Burl: 1833-1900 Dún na Sí; 1877-1900 WL (index)

Civil Parish: Newtown
CoI Parish: Newtownfertullagh
Bapt: 1889-1989 RCBL
Marr: 1846-1980 RCBL
Burl: 1889-1994 RCBL

CoI Parish: Portnashangan
Bapt: 1878-1983 RCBL; 1877-1900 SLC film 1279272 indexed; 1878-1899 Dun na Sí; 1879-1899 WL (index)
Marr: 1846-1979 RCBL; 1846-1900 SLC film 1279272 indexed; 1846-1879 Dun na Sí; 1846-1879 WL (index)
Burl: 1880-1977 RCBL; 1877-1900 SLC film 1279272 indexed; 1880-1900 Dun na Sí; 1880-1900 WL (index)

CoI Parish: Rathaspick
Bapt: 1807-1900 Dun na Sí HC
Marr: 1850-1877 Dun na Sí HC

CoI Parish: Rathconnell
Bapt: 1881-1953 RCBL
Marr: 1845-1895 RCBL
Burl: 1881-1895 RCBL

Civil Parish: Rathgarve
CoI Parish: Castlepollard
Marr: 1845-1953 RCBL

CoI Parish: Stonehall
Bapt: 1814-1941 RCBL; 1814-57 NAI MFCI 62
Marr: 1814-1912 RCBL: 1814-54 NAI MFCI 62
Burl: 1815-1979 RCBL; 1915-54 NAI MFCI 62

CoI Parish: Streete
Bapt: 1827-1899 Dún na Sí
Marr: 1827-1898 Dún na Sí
Burial: 1827-1899 Dún na Sí

CoI Parish: Taghmon
Marr: 1832-1867 Dún na Sí: 1848-1869 WL (index)
Burl: 1878-1900 Dún na Sí

Civil Parish: St. Feighin's
CoI Parish: Collinstown
Bapt: 1838-1963 RCBL; NAI MFCI 51
Marr: 1838-1963 RCBL; 1818-51 NAI MFCI 51
Burl: 1837-1967 RCBL; 1837-1960 NAI MFCI 51

Civil Parish: St. Mary's Athlone
CoI Parish: Athlone St. Mary's
Bapt: 1768-1999 RCBL; 1849-1903 NLI Pos 5309; 1746 NAI MFC1
57; 1834-1881 Dún na Sí; 1842-46 SLC film 1279272 and 4; 3.1747-
1.1849; 1849-90 BP
Marr: 1767-1956 RCBL; 1845-90 NLI Pos 5309; 1746 NAI MFC1 57;
1835-60 SLC film 1279272 and 4; 3.1747-1.1849; 1845-90 BP
Burl: 1747-1892 RCBL; 1849-1888 NLI Pos 5309; 1746 NAI
MFC1 57; 1786-1875 Dun na Sí HC; 1710-1896 SLC film 1279272
and 4: 3.1747-1.1849; 1849-71 BP
Vestry Book 1750-1888 NLI p.5309; BP.

Civil Parish: St. Mary's Athlone
CoI Parish: Willbrook (Moydrum)
Bapt: 1756-83 RCBL; NLI Pos. 5309; NAI MFCI 62: Dún na Sí;
1756-83 SLC film 1279272; 1756-1783 BP.
Marr: 1775-1954 RCBL; 1763-75 NLI Pos. 5309; 1763-1775 Dún na
Sí; 1763-1775 BP.

CoI Parish: St. Peter's Athlone
Marr: 1845-70 NLI p.5309
Vestry minutes 1846-1941

Vestry Minute Books
Vestry Minute Books survive for some Church of Ireland parishes at
the RCBL and they may be useful to genealogists as they sometimes
contain baptism, marriage and burial entries and frequently contain
names of church wardens, those confirmed, names of the poor, widows
and orphans receiving relief and names of overseers of the poor and

of public works. They may also contain names of cess payers (cess was the name given to a local tax levied by the general vestry for the maintenance of the roads, etc.)

Other Denominations

Other religious denominations with communities in Westmeath are: Presbyterian, Methodists, Baptists, Huguenots, Congregationalists and Quakers. The background to these churches and their records is also outlined in *Irish Church Records*, Flyleaf Press and in Brian Mitchell, *A Guide to Irish Parish Registers*, Baltimore, 1988. Records for Methodists, Baptists and Congregationalists may sometimes be found in local custody or within the parish registers of the Church of Ireland. The 1861 census shows that Baptists, Society of Friends or Quakers tended to be located in the Baronies of Brawny and Clonlonan.

Civil Parish: St. Mary's Athlone
Athlone Methodist Church
Bapt; 1842-1900 BP; 1842-1900 Dún na Sí
Marr; 1866-1941 BP; 1866-1896 Dún na Sí
Burial: 1808-1849 Dún na Sí

Civil Parish: Kilcleagh 1
Moate Quaker Cemetery
Death: 1816-1900 Dún na Sí; Liam Cox, *Moate County Westmeath; a history of The Town and District, Athlone*, 1981, page 230. Liam Cox et al *Moate Quaker Cemetery, Moate,* 1985.

Chapter 7   Land Records

Until relatively recent times, Ireland was primarily an agricultural country and access to land was of major economic importance. There are therefore a wide range of records which deal with ownership, occupancy, sale and rental of land. These records can play a major role in the search for your roots. Because land was a major economic asset, it was also a basis for taxation both by the State and by the Church. The process of estimating and collecting these land-based taxes created two major sources of records (Tithe Applotments and Valuation records). For historical reasons, the structure of Irish land tenure was that vast tracts of land were given to individuals in return for services to the British Crown. The land on these estates was typically rented out. In some cases it was leased to smaller landlords, who often rented it to smallholders. Therefore the occupiers, or holders, of the land were generally not the owners but small farmers and cottiers. Many of these land-holders had no legal agreement for their holding and were 'tenants at will'. Where leases existed they could be for the period of the lives of the persons specified on the lease or for a particular period of time. The records of these transactions, where they exist, are of major significance to the researcher. They are however, private records of landlords, and many have not come into the public domain.

When a townland is identified as being the home of your ancestor and its location found using the Townland Index described on page 26, the next step is to link the name with the place in whatever official records are available. You must never assume an entry for the name of interest is your ancestral line. The same family names will occur many times in an area. Cross-checking civil and church records with what is known usually clarifies matters. The dates known to you will determine the best place to start looking for information. The following are some land records that are frequently used by researchers:

Tithe Applotment Books

Tithes were a tax for the maintenance of the Church of Ireland (see page 73). Prior to 1823 tithes were paid in kind, i.e. agricultural produce. However, the Tithe Composition Act (1823) permitted clergymen to negotiate a fixed, twice-yearly payment. Tithes were legally payable by land-holders of all denominations, but in practice only by land holders of certain types of land (typically tilled land). It is therefore not a comprehensive listing of all households in an area. The Tithe Applotment Books are a record of tithes due. Each record gives the name of the landholder, quantity of land (and quality), portion deemed titheable and the amount payable. The Tithe Books for Westmeath are dated approximately 1824-35. Originals are held at the NAI and copies are available on microfilm at NAI, NLI and WL. The quality of the records is very variable. Tithe Collection Books for earlier periods occasionally survive: those for 1805-12 for Saint Mary's Parish, Athlone are, for example, appended to the 1824 Books for the Parish. The NLI has an index to householder's in Griffith's Valuation (see below) and the Tithe Applotment Books. An Index to the Tithe Applotment Books may be searched online at the subscription site www.ancestry.co.uk - see page 83.

A typescript copy of the Castlepollard Tithe records transcribed by Micheál Ó Conláin is available for reference at WL. A digitized copy of the Tithe Applotment Book for Leany, Templeoran, Kilbixy and Rathaspick dated 1820 – 1821 is available for public access at WL.

Griffith's Valuation

The Primary Valuation of Ireland (or Griffith's Valuation) was carried out countrywide between 1848 and 1864 by teams of surveyors under the direction of Richard Griffith. Its purpose was to determine how much tax, (commonly called 'rates') each property-holder was liable to pay. The tax was based on an estimation, or valuation, of the productive potential of all land and property. Arranged by poor law union, barony, civil parish and townland, it lists the occupier's name (head of household), the immediate lessor (if the occupier was paying rent to another person), description of the holding, location (townland, civil parish etc), amount and quality and total valuation. It also provides a map reference to the location of the property on a valuation map. It is not a total record of all inhabitants of an area, but does list heads of households occupying property – even simple cottages without a

Townland of Russagh, continued, Parish of Russagh & Barony

No	Occupiers Names	Whole Quantity in Statute Acres	First Quality	Second Quality	Third Quality	Vicarial Amt of Rate Charge	Impropriate Amt of Rate Charge
8	James Nugent & Michael Nugent	21.2.22	19.6.00	2.2.22	—	0.11.9	1.3.9
9	Michael Nugent do. do.	21.2.22	19.6.00	2.2.22	—	0.15.3	1.3.9
		£18.0.6				£6.12.5½	

Townland of Lower Loughanstown, Parish of Russagh & Barony of Moyas

No	Occupiers Names	Whole Quantity in Statute Acres	First Quality	Second Quality	Third Quality	Vicarial Amt of Rate Charge	Impropriate Amt of Rate Charge
1	Francis Nugent	12..0.00	4..0.00	1..2.00	6..2.00	0..4.10½	0..7..7
2	Michael Nugent	12..0.00	3..2.00	3..2.00	5..0.00	0..4.11½	0..7..8
3	Barth'y Sherridan	12..0.00	3..0.00	5..2.00	3..2.00	0..5..00	0..7.10
4	James Wildman	9..2.14	4..2.14	4..0.00	1..0.00	0..5.12	0..8..0
5	William Hamstrong	19..1.30	9..1.30	8..0.00	2..0.00	0..10.5½	0..16..4
6	Peter Green	9..2.00	4..2.00	4..0.00	1..0.00	0..5..1	0..7.10
7	Widow Connell	1..1.00	1..1.00	—	—	0..0.11	0..1..5
8	Bryan Sheeran	6..0.00	6..0.00	—	—	0..4..6	0..7..0

An extract from the *Tithe Applotment Book for the townlands of Russagh and Lower Loughanstown* - see page 82

(Courtesy of Westmeath County Library)

yard or garden. It is an almost complete record of heads of households in the case of property located in the countryside. It also records all householders in towns except tenement buildings, i.e. buildings which housed a number of families, when the head of one of those families will generally be recorded.

The survey is invaluable as there are virtually no surviving census records for the 1848/64 period. A significant additional advantage is that the original record was updated, in books known as Cancelled Valuation Books, whenever there was a change of occupier or lessor or an increase or reduction in the value of the original property. By referring to the Cancelled Valuation Books, the succession to the property can be ascertained down to recent times. Such succession information, cross-referenced against the known children of the individuals involved, and against the 1901 and 1911 Censuses for the townland in question, will usually remove whatever doubts there may be, if any, as to the identities of the families listed in the original survey. The Cancelled Valuation Books are in manuscript, containing deletions and insertions, and can sometimes be difficult to decipher. The original survey records, together with the associated Cancelled Books, nevertheless constitute an ongoing record of heads of household nationwide from the middle of the 19th century. The Cancelled Valuation Books are available for inspection, for a fee, in the Valuation Office, Dublin.

The original surveyors inspected each property and building and used three different notebooks to compile their information. These can be found in the NAI. The House Books contain a more detailed description of each house and outbuilding, showing dimensions and, sometimes, a sketch. As House Books, in particular, were prepared some years before the survey of land was completed, they may show an earlier occupier of the property than in the final, published, survey. The Field Books and Tenure Books also sometimes contain additional information. A number of valuation books for c.1900 and c.1950 are in the archives at WL. Microfilm copies of these records are available at the local studies department of WL. Griffith's Valuation Survey records are also available free of charge at www.askaboutireland.ie and at www.originsnetwork.com where for a small sum one can view the original records and print an entry. Online access is provided free of charge at the NLI. The 'Householders' index of surnames for Westmeath is available at the NLI and WL, and is an index of all persons in the

PARISH OF RATHASPICK.

No. and Letters of reference to Map.	Townlands and Occupiers.	Immediate Lessors.	Description of Tenement.	Area. A. R. P.	Rateable Annual Valuation. Land £ s. d.	Buildings £ s. d.	Total Annual Valuation of Rateable Property. £ s. d.
	RATHOWEN—*continued.* TOWN OF RATHOWEN.						
a	Reps. Sir Geo. Fetherston and Eliz. Westby,	Reps. Sir Geo. Fetherston & Eliz. Westby,	Petit sessions' court, *Half rent received for Petit sessions' court, £2 10s.*			2 0 0	2 0 0
26	Peter Grace,	Matthew Torney,	House,	—	—	0 10 0	0 10 0
27	Edward Farrell,	Same,	House,	—	—	1 0 0	1 0 0
28	Bernard Clancey,	Reps. Sir Geo. Fetherston & Eliz. Westby,					
29	William Madden,	Same,	Office (*forge*),	0 1 8	0 10 0	0 10 0	1 0 0
30	Patrick Mehady,	Same,	Ho., off., yard, & garden,	0 1 8	0 10 0	1 0 0	1 10 0*
31	Thomas Fullham,	Same,	Ho., off., yard, & garden,	0 0 23	0 5 0	1 0 0	1 0 0
32	William Robinson,	Same,	House, office. & garden,	0 1 0	0 10 0	0 15 0	1 10 0
33	George Young,	Same,	House and garden,	0 1 0	0 10 0	1 5 0	1 5 0
34	William M'Loughlin,	Same,	House and garden,	0 0 18	0 5 0	1 5 0	1 10 0
35	John Malone,	Thomas Moran,	House,			2 10 0	2 10 0
36	Thomas Moran,	Same,					
37	Edward Connolly,	Reps. Sir G. Fetherston and Elizabeth Westby,	House and garden,	0 0 25	0 5 0	2 0 0	2 5 0
38	William Dardis,	Thomas Moran,	House,	—	—	0 8 0	0 8 0
39	John Swift,	Same,	House,	—	—	0 8 0	0 8 0
40	Patrick Phylan,	Reps. Sir G. Fetherston and Elizabeth Westby,	House,				
41	Matthew M'Keon,	Matthew Torney,	House,	0 0 15	0 3 0	1 10 0	1 10 0
			House, office, & garden,			2 12 0	2 15 0

An extract from *Griffith's Valuation of the town of Rathowen* - see page 82.

Valuation. It shows the number of times a surname appears in each parish and barony and which union book to consult. It also states if the surname appears in the Tithe Applotment Books. It can be useful in determining the distribution of a particular name within the county.

Valuation maps are the maps which correspond to the above valuation. The originals are held in the Valuation Office, Dublin. Scanned images of valuation maps and later maps c.1900 are available on-line at www. valoff.ie (see page 150).Valuation maps may also be viewed at www. askaboutireland.ie Used in conjunction with Griffith's Valuation Survey, it may be possible to identify the location of an ancestral holding.

Registry of Deeds.
A deed is the written, signed and witnessed, record of an agreement between two or more people or institutions. The majority of deeds deal with property transactions e.g. leases, mortgages and conveyances, and also marriage settlements. They tend to be more relevant to landed families. The Registry of Deeds was established in 1708 for the purpose of registering such deeds. It is located in the Kings Inns, Henrietta Street, Dublin. For a fee the public has access to the records. Official copies of a memorial (i.e. a synopsis) may also be ordered. A search of the records is time consuming, the books are very heavy and many are on high shelves. However the results can be very rewarding. There are two indices available to the researcher, as follows:

Grantor's Index. This is an alphabetical index of the names of grantors (the person who sold or leased the property). The index is for grantors in all counties and it gives no indication of address or location of the grantor (or the property) up to 1833. After 1833 the county in which the land was situated is shown and this enhances searchability. There is no alphabetical index to grantees (the persons who received the property), therefore if the name of the grantor is not known the land index must be used.

Land Index. The index to lands is arranged by county, and then by initial letter of each townland: however it is not in any further alphabetical order. The second column is intended to show the barony but this is not always the case. To check on the availability of a deed, it is necessary to check all of the townlands of possible relevance to your family. After

1828 the county index is divided into baronies. The index to grantors and the land index is available on microfilm in the NLI. P.2001-P.2408

Deeds can be useful to the researcher but they were usually drawn up by people of wealth. However, others may be mentioned as witnesses, listed tenants, neighbours (lands are often defined according to the neighbouring properties) or relatives of the parties to the deed. Small collections of Deeds are also to be found in the NLI, NAI, the Royal Irish Academy, Trinity College Dublin, the Public Record Office of Northern Ireland, in estate collections, solicitor's papers and in local archives and County Libraries, some of which may not be registered.

Encumbered Estates (or Incumbered Estates)

The Encumbered Estates Court (later the Landed Estates Court) was established under the Encumbered Estates Act of 1849 to facilitate the sale of insolvent estates by their bankrupt owners. Brochures and promotional documents relating to these sales usually give the name of the person to whom the current lease of the property was issued, often in the 18th century, and the names of those who have since succeeded to the lease, together with any family members or other persons cited in the term of the lease. They will also usually include tenant's names and, where the tenant had a long-term lease, will often include the names of other family members as many such leases were for the lives of the tenant and named family members. Landed Estates Court documents are held at the NAI., e.g. Encumbered Estate court Rental of the Estate of the Earl of Mornington in Kings County, Queens County, Dublin, Meath, Westmeath and Cavan for sale, Dec. 11th, 1863, NAI M.6186. The Encumbered Estate Court records are available for online searching at the subscription website www.findmypast.ie.

The Land Commission

The Land Commission was set up by the Land Act of 1881 to regulate land rental practices, which had previously strongly favoured landlords. It also had the power to purchase insolvent or abandoned estates and transfer them to viable owners, usually the sitting tenants. It was a major force in the massive transfer of land ownership from landlord to small farmer which occurred from the 1880s up to the 1950s. In the 1930s, 40s and 50s the Land Commission also looked after the transfer of families from western counties to land holdings in the midland counties including Westmeath. The Land Commission records which deal with the dissolution of large estates in the late nineteenth and early twentieth century and in the redistribution of the land are housed in the same building as the NAI. At time of writing they are not freely accessible to the researcher however a written request by a direct descendant of a person referred to in the records may yield results. Land Commission card indices: (1) by estate and (2) by vendor and also a card index to wills held by the Land Commission are available in the reading room at the NLI.

The Land Registry
The Land Registry was established in 1892 to provide a system of compulsory registration of land title. When a title was registered relevant details concerning description, ownership and burden were recorded under a folio number. The Land Registry holds maps relating to all registrations. The index for each county shows the folio number(s) corresponding to each name. All title registrations and map records for Westmeath are held by the Land Registry, Chancery Street, Dublin 7. Details of the Land Registry can be found at www.landregistry.ie .

There are also earlier Land records. These usually do not provide genealogical information but may nonetheless give an insight into the geographical distribution of names as far back as the seventeenth century. They include:

Down Survey
After the Cromwellian victory of the early 1650s, vast amounts of land were confiscated and distributed to the adventurers and soldiers who either provided money to the English Parliament for the war in Ireland, or were members of the parliamentary armies. The Down Survey was carried out by Dr. William Petty to measure the confiscated lands. It was known as The Down Survey because it was laid down on maps. (See 'The Books of Survey and Distribution page 38). The Down Survey maps, also known as the Petty maps, give details such as boundaries, placenames and acreages with accompanying descriptions. Copies exist for the twelve baronies in Westmeath at a scale of 160 perches per inch and are available at NLI and WL. The Down Survey parish maps NLI Ref. P.7384, (microfilm) are divided into plots and are accompanied by a description under the headings: Number in plot, Proprietors Names, Denomination of Lands, Numbers of Acres by Administration, Lands Profitable and Lands Unprofitable.

Fiants (1500s)
'Fiant' is the shortened version of 'Fiant literae patentes' which means 'Let letters Patent be made' and are the warrants relating to the granting of lands, pardons etc. by the government. The fiants themselves do not survive but calendars of fiants of Henry VIII, Edward VI, Mary and Elizabeth are printed in *Reports of the Deputy Keeper of the Public Record Office*. They have been republished by Éamonn de Búrca - The Irish Fiants of the Tudor Sovereigns during the Reigns of Henry VIII, Edward VI, Philip and Mary, and Elizabeth I, 4 vols., Dublin, 1994. Originally published in The Twenty-First Report of the DKPRI [22nd May, 1889].
The following is an example of the type of information that can be found in the Calendars:
'2710 (2168.) Pardon to Wm. Tute, of Tutestone, co. Westmeath,Esq., sheriff of the county, Walter Tute, of same, gent. his brother,Edw. Pettit, of Bellena, same co., gent., Rich. Tute, of Tutestoun,Gent., and Laurence mac William Fitzgerald, of Barrye, co. Longford, Horseman. – 20 Sept., xvii'.

Calendar of the Patent and Close Rolls of Chancery in Ireland (1500s)
Patent and Close Rolls contain the letters patent authorized in the fiants. They were called patent because they were open to the inspection of all. The Close Rolls contain liberates, writs, pardons, etc. James Morrin, Editor, Calendar of the Patent and Close Rolls of Chancery in Ireland, of the reigns of Henry VIII, Edward VI., Mary, and Elizabeth, 2 volumes, Dublin, 1861. The following is an entry from the Patent and Close Rolls in the reign of Henry VIII: *'Grant to Edward Field of Cousingeston, Patrick Clinch of Skryne, and Philip Penteney of Tanaght, gentlemen, of the late monastery of house of Friars Observant of Multyfarnane, and all its possessions, in the county of Westmeath; To hold in capite by knights's service, that is, by the twentieth part of a knight's fee, at a rent of 4s. – April 5, 37'.*

Calendar of Documents Relating to Ireland
The Calendar of Documents Relating to Ireland, 1171-1301, lists all the instruments and entries relating to Ireland in the Public Records of England. They give information relating to grants of land, the right to hold a fair and other administrative issues. They can be searched in H.S. Sweetman, Editor, Calendar of Documents relating to Ireland 1171-1301, 4 volumes, London, 1875-1881.

Calendar of State Papers Relating to Ireland

The Calendar of State Papers relating to Ireland, 1509-1670 contain grants, orders for letters patent, petitions and other administrative issues. The volume Robert Pentland Mahaffy, Editor, Calendar of the State Papers relating to Ireland in The Public Record Office; Adventurers for Land, 1642-1659, London, 1903 is particularly interesting because it lists the receipts given to persons who subscribed money for the support of the Parliamentary cause in Ireland in the years 1642, 1643 and 1647, in return for the promise of land in Ireland. It also lists the documents by which their heirs, executors and administrators proved their right to claim lands in Ireland in the years 1653 and 1654. It can be viewed on the open shelves in the reading room of the NLI.

Estate Records

The vast majority of the population in the eighteenth and nineteenth century were small tenant farmers on large estates owned by English or Anglo-Irish landlords. The running of these estates necessitated the keeping of records e.g. rent books, leases, account books, etc. Estate records are held in various national and local archives and some still remain in private hands. Surviving family members may have such documents, or may be able to identify the solicitor that dealt with the estate. Where they do survive they vary in regard to the quality and quantity of rentals, maps, deeds, wage books or letters which survive, and in their content. To establish whether estate papers exist for an area of interest (typically for the estate on which an ancestor was a tenant), the first step for the researcher is to identify the landlord. This can be done by checking one of the following sources, all of which indicate major landlords in each area:

(i) 'Immediate Lessors' column of Griffith's Valuation. This lists the person to whom the occupier paid a rent. However, this person may only be an intermediary landlord who paid a rent in turn to another. It is useful to keep a watchful eye on the 'Occupier' column in order to spot if an 'Immediate Lessor' is in turn the tenant of another 'Immediate Lessor'.

(ii) Land Owners in Ireland, Return of Owners of land of one acre and Upwards, in the Several Counties, Counties of Cities, and Counties of Towns in Ireland, Dublin, 1876. This may be searched online from the subscription site www.ancestry.co.uk

LAND OWNERS IN IRELAND.

RETURN OF OWNERS OF LAND

OF

ONE ACRE AND UPWARDS,

IN THE SEVERAL

COUNTIES, COUNTIES OF CITIES, AND COUNTIES OF TOWNS

IN IRELAND,

Showing the names of such Owners arranged Alphabetically in each County; their addresses—as far as could be ascertained—the extent in Statute Acres, and the Valuation in each case; together with the number of Owners in each County of less than One Statute Acre in extent; and the total Area and Valuation of such properties; and the Grand Total of Area and Valuation for all Owners of property in each County, County of a City, or County of a Town.

TO WHICH IS ADDED

A SUMMARY FOR EACH PROVINCE AND FOR ALL IRELAND.

Presented to both Houses of Parliament by Command of Her Majesty.

GENEALOGICAL PUBLISHING CO., INC.

Baltimore   *1988*

see *Land Owners in Ireland* on opposite page

(iii) U.H. Husssey de Burgh, *The Landowners of Ireland 1878.* An Alphabetical List of the Owners of Estates of 500 Acres or £500 Valuation and upwards, in Ireland, with the Acreage and Valuation in each County, Dublin, no date (see below).

Name, Titles, and Addresses.	County.	Acreage.	Valuation. £
BATTERSBY, GEORGE, LL.D., Q.C. Educated at Trin. Coll. Dublin; J.P. cos. Meath, Westmeath, Cavan, and Monaghan; Chancellor of the United Diocese of Dublin, Glendalough, and Kildare; was Judge of the Provincial Court of Dublin, 1864-71,—Lough Bawn, Collinstown, co. Westmeath; 20 Lr. Leeson st., Dublin; Kildare Street Club, Dublin.	Cavan - Meath - Westmeath - Wexford -	* * 576 331 439 1346	82 479 225 373 1159
BATTY, Rev. EDWARD, M.A., Ballyhealy, Delvin. [Rental, £920.]	Westmeath -	1215	748
BATTY, EDWARD, Dundee, N.B.	Mayo - -	2151	629
BATTY, Mrs. FRANCIS H., Ashbank House, Blairgowrie, N.B.	Queen's -	625	321
BAXTER, EDWARD, Dundee, N.B.	Mayo - -	2151	629
BAXTER, Mrs. FRANCIS H., Ashbrook House, Blairgowrie, N.B.	Queen's -	625	321
BAYLEE, Mrs. SUSANNA, Anna Villa, Templeogue, Dublin.	Clare - -	910	626
BAYLEY, EDWARD, Dublin.	Westmeath -	989	466
BAYLEY, Reps. of the late ROBERT PRESTON, J.P. and D.L. co. Roscommon; J.P. co. Galway; (High Sheriff, 1869); was a Member of the Royal College of Surgeons,—Rookwood, Athleague, co. Roscommon.	Galway - Roscommon- Westmeath -	294 2590 284 3168	200 1757 194 2151
BAYLY, Col. EDWARD SYMES. Educated at Harrow; J.P. and D.L. co. Wicklow (High Sheriff, 1837); late Lieut.-Col. Com. Wicklow Militia, and formerly Capt. 34th Foot,—Ballyarthur, Ovoca; Kildare St. Club, Dublin.	Westmeath - Wicklow -	659 3026 3685	139 1872 2011

Entries from *The Landowners of Ireland, 1878* - see above.

(iv) John Bateman, *The Great Landowners of Great Britain and Ireland,* 4th edition, New York, 1970.

(v) Samuel A Lewis, *Topographical Dictionary of Ireland,* 3 volumes, London, 1837. This resource is available for online seaching and reading, without charge, at www.libraryireland.com

(vi) John Charles Lyons, *The Grand Juries of the County of Westmeath from the year 1727 to the year 1853,* 2 volumes in one, Ledeston, 1853. Accessible on line at www.askaboutireland.ie

The next step is to establish if there are any records and if so where they are located. There are a number of ways to do this. Manuscript Sources for the History of Irish Civilisation, edited by Richard Hayes, Boston, 1965, (First Supplement, 1965-75, Boston, 1979) is a good place to start. It is available at http://sources.nli.ie and in most major Irish-interest libraries. You may check under the name of the landlord or the name of the place where the estate was located. If a document exists, the index will provide a brief description of the manuscript, the manuscript number and the archive in which it is available. The NLI and the NAI are continually building their on-line catalogues which are available at their respective web pages. At each archive a search of the card catalogues and the finding aids which are available in the reading rooms of both these repositories is a must. One finding-aid specific to Westmeath is Helen Kelly, Estate Papers in the National Library and National Archives, Co. Westmeath, [Dublin], 2003 (typescript). WL holds some estate papers the largest of which is the Howard Bury Collection. Smaller collections include papers relating to the Clibborn, Reynell and Meares families. *The Big Houses and Landed Estates of Ireland – a research guide* by Terence Dooley (Four Courts Press, 2007) is also an excellent source for the family history researcher.

Estate Maps
Landowners surveyed their property for many reasons varying from establishing exactly what they owned, to managing leases and sales. The surveying of estates in Ireland dates back to the 1590s and most of these surveys would have been professionally undertaken. A search of estate papers in the NLI and other repositories often reveals sketch maps of holdings attached to leasing agreements showing the lessees name and the names of those with adjoining leases. A good example

is the O'Hara papers in the NLI, which contain many maps. A check under maps in http://sources.nli.ie or the subject volume of Hayes's Manuscript Sources gives a full list of maps and surveys for County Westmeath.

Westmeath library has digitised eighty eight estate maps with a date range c.1761 to c.1914 from their holdings which includes a Survey of the estates of Abraham Boyd Esquire and the Countess of Belvedere in the county of Westmeath (1818). Most maps have an accompanying table which gives the map reference, landlord's name, townland where estate is located and scale of the map. The list of tenant names appearing on these maps varies from one or two names to 96 names.

George Taylor and Andrew Skinner, *Taylor and Skinner's Maps of the Roads of Ireland, surveyed 1777,* London/Dublin, 1778 illustrates and gives names of large landowners only and therefore is limited in use to the researcher except insofar as identifying the location of an estate an ancestor might have lived or worked on.

William Larkin, *A Survey of the County Westmeath with a sketch of the adjacent Country*, London, 1808 shows the big houses and usually the names of the families therein. In line with Taylor's and Skinner's maps it is more relevant to the landed class.

For a full account of the various maps resulting from nineteenth century surveys Jacinta Prunty, *Maps and Map-making in Local History,* Dublin, 2004 and J.H. Andrews, *A Paper Landscape, the Ordnance Survey in Nineteenth-Century Ireland,* 2nd ed., Dublin, 2002 are but two of the many titles available on the subject.

The landed Estates database compiled by NUI Galway may be searched on line, without charge at www.landedestates.nuigalway.ie While this project so far only covers estates in the counties of Connacht and Munster a small number of Westmeath families owned land in this area and they are included.

Chapter 8

Wills, Administrations and Marriage Bonds

A will is a person's final instructions as to how they want their assets distributed after their death. It can provide a clear picture of relationships, and also of properties associated with a family. The maker of the will (the testator) will usually specify the names of spouses, children, siblings and other relatives receiving property. The testator will also appoint a trusted person (the executor) to carry out their instructions and this too may prove a useful lead. In order to achieve legal status, a will must be 'proven' by a Probate Court.

Administration takes place when the deceased made no will (i.e. they were intestate) or if the will is otherwise inoperable, for instance, the executor is also deceased. In this case the Probate Court will decide how the property of a deceased person is distributed based on current legal principle and natural justice.

Original wills and administrations.
Although the major collection of Irish wills was destroyed in the Public Record Office fire in 1922, The National Archives still has the largest national collection of wills, including copies and abstracts of some of those destroyed. This was put together from wills stored in other archives, as well as from private collections. Wills are also to be found in the Registry of Deeds, the Representative Church Body Library and to a lesser extent the Society of Friends Library and the Irish Genealogical Research Society, London.

Background to the Administration of Wills

Before starting to locate a will you need to familiarise yourself with the authorities under which probate was conducted, the types of wills under these authorities and the timeframes during which these authorities operated (See the table below).

Timeframe	Administrative Authority	
	Types of Probate Court	
To the end of 1857	*Church of Ireland*	
	Prerogative Will	Consistorial Will
	State Authority	
From 1858 to date	**Types of Probate Court**	
	Principal Will	District Will

Wills to the end of 1857

Prior to 1858, the Church of Ireland, being the Established Church, was responsible for probate administration and had a court system for this purpose. Wills were proven in either the Prerogative Court in Armagh, or in a Diocesan (or Consistorial) court in a particular diocese.

Prerogative Wills

Prerogative Wills were those which involved distribution of property exceeding £5 in a second Diocese. These had to be dealt with in the Prerogative Court under the jurisdiction of the Archbishop of Armagh. They relate mainly to the wealthier classes. However, those whose property straddled a diocesan border may also have their wills proven in this court. All original prerogative wills were destroyed so the researcher must use the details which can be gleaned from surviving indexes, abstracts, grants and will books.

Surviving Material of the Prerogative Court
Indexes to Prerogative Wills

Time frame	Reference / Location
1484 - 1858	CD - *Index of Irish Wills* www.eneclann.ie and www.findmypast.ie
1536 –1810	Arthur Vicars, Index to the Prerogative Wills of Ireland, 1536 –1810, Dublin, 1897 and NAI
1811 - 1858	Manuscript - NAI and PRONI

1760	**Tuite**,	John, Dublin, vintner
1728	,,	sir Joseph, Sonna, co. Westmeath, bart.
1749	,,	dame Mary
1780	,,	Mary, Dublin, shopkeeper
1782	,,	Mary, Henry-street, Dublin, widow
1804	,,	Patience, Dublin city, widow
1719	,,	Patrick, Corvanstown, co. Kildare, gent.
1689	,,	Philip, Newcastle, co. Westmeath, esq.
1778	,,	Philip, Newcastle, co. Westmeath, esq.
1758	**Tuke**,	Francis, Drakestown, co. Meath, gent.
1790	,,	Francis, Causetown, co. Meath, esq.
1806	,,	James, Dublin city
1803	,,	Mary, Eccles-st., Dubl., wid.
1810	**Tullekin**,	Rachel, Sundays Well, Cork, widow
1782	**Tully**,	Anne, *alias* **Coffy**, Belin, co. Westmeath, gentlewoman
1740	,,	Hillary, par. St. Martin, Middlesex, but in Carolina
1810	,,	James, Dublin city
1757	,,	John, Kilcock, co. Kildare, M.D.
1794	,,	John, Loughrea, co. Galway, esq.
1706	,,	Laghlen, Cormanagh, co. Westmeath, glazier
1760	,,	Loughlin, Ballenamulle, co. Roscommon
1704	,,	Marcus, Dublin, gent.
1742	,,	Mathew, Limerick, gent.
1748	,,	Mathew, Gortnagrange, co. Roscommon, glazier
1811	,,	Ross, Athlone, co. Westmeath

An extract from
Index to the Prerogative Wills of Ireland, 1536 –1810
- see page 96.

Prerogative Will Books

Source	Surviving Material and Location
Will Books	1664-1684; 1706-1708, 1726-1729 (A-W); 1777 (A-L); 1813 (A-Z); 1834 (A-E) - NAI, also in Testamentary Card Index.
Grants	1684-1688; 1748-1751; 1839 - NAI
Day Books	1784-1788 - NAI

Diocesan Wills

Diocesan Wills were those which referred to property in one diocese only. In these cases probate was granted at the local Consistorial Court under the charge of the bishop. The diocesan wills for Westmeath were proven in the diocese of either Meath or Ardagh. The indexes to the diocesan wills typically list the testator, date of death and of probate and sometimes specify a residence.

Surviving Material of the Diocesan Courts for Westmeath
Indexes to Diocesan Wills

Diocese	Time frame / Location
Ardagh	1695-1858 NAI, also Ir.Anc. (Supplement) 1971
Meath	1572-1858 (fragments and transcripts) NAI

Index to Diocesan Administration Bonds

Diocese	Time frame / Location
Ardagh	1697-1850 - NAI
Meath	1663-1857 - NAI

Will Abstracts:

The basic information in many wills has been abstracted for a variety of legal and family reasons. Chief among these sources is the Betham Abstracts. In 1810 Sir William Betham, Ulster King of Arms, superintended the construction of an alphabetical index to testators on behalf of the Record Commissioners. (Betham Abstracts, National Archives, MFGS 38/1-32). He also wrote a brief genealogical abstract and later constructed sketch pedigrees from his notes. They are in the NAI and at the NLI, G.O. Mss. 223-254. Commonly referred to as 'Betham's Abstracts' they are of immense value to the researcher.

McManus John, Graffogue, 1824
    Owen P., Greeg(—), Co. Roscommon, 1708
    Owen, Ballirhillin, Co. Cavan, 1787
    Thomas, Graffouge, Co. Lfd., 1843
McNaboy Teig, Crumra, Co. Lfd., 1706-7
McNamarrow Thomas, Corrocraugh, Cloon, 1813
McNeil Arthur, Aughadruminshin, 1826
McNerhany Patrick, Greagh, Co. Lfd., 1813
McNerheny Henry, Ballycross, Abbeylara, 1816
McQuead Patrick, Brenrosscullagh, Co. Lfd., 1796
McRann Patrick, Corraick, Co. Lt., 1810
McVitty John, Cartrons, Co. Lfd., 1785

Nanny or Nannery Richard, Curracreehan, Co. Lfd., 1830
Nanry John, Barry, Co. Lfd., 1840
Nedly John, Bonnybrook, Street, 1752
Newcomen James, Carriglass, Co. Lfd., 1770
    James, Templemichael, Co. Lfd., 1776
Newland John, Meenaghan, Co. Lt., 1833
    William, Gurteen, Co. Lt., 1813
Newman Bryan, Cartrawar, Co. Lfd., 1810
Newton Moses, Barry, Co. Lfd., 1832
Nicholson John, Clooncavil, Co. Lfd., 1767
Nicolls Archibald, Granard, Co. Lfd., 1815
    Archibald, Rossou, Co. Lt., 1840
    Peter, Bohy, Co. Lt., 1797
    Susan, 1851
Nightengele Robert, Longford, 1752
Nightingal Margaret, Longford, 1762
Nixon Adam, Cranly Begg, 1721
    Robert, Cranallaghbeg, Co. Lfd., 1754
    Samuel, 1849
Noble Andrew, Abbydarrag, 1786
Norris Richard, Rathmore, Co. Lfd., 1834
Nowlan Catherine, Carrickedmond, Co. Lfd., 1856
    James, Aughnashougan, Co. Lfd., 1808
    Timothy, Corry, Co. Lfd., 1808
Nugent Andrew, Barratogher, Co. Westmeath, 1790
    Dominick, Rossagh, Co. Westmeath, 1794

Nugent Elizabeth, Coolamber, Co. Westmeath, 1709
    John, Killosoma, Co, Lfd., 1707-8
    Michael, Gub Cormongan, Co. Lt., 1819
    Richard, Aughenagarron, Co. Lfd., 1701
    Thomas, Coolamber, Co. Westmeath, *1695
O'Beirne Frances, James Town Lodge, Co. Lt., 1829
O'Brian James, Corunullo, Co. Lt., 1765
O'Brien Thomas, Largan, Co. Lt., 1814
O'Bryan David, Cornollow, Co. Lt., 1739
O'Connell, Bridget, Cromary, 1808
    Philip, Gelshaugh, 1811
O'Connor Patrick, Clundra, Co. Lfd., *1780
    Patrick, 1851
O'Donohoe James (Rev. P.P.), Longford, 1846
O'Ferrall Dominick, Ballimee, Co. Lfd., 1816
    John (Rev.), P.P. of Carrickedmond, 1800
O'Hara Arthur, Bonlahy, Co. Lfd., 1812
    Henry, Lisduff, Co. Westmeath, 1834
    Joseph, Lisduff, Co. Westmeath, 1834
    Mathew, Bawn, Co. Lfd., 1847
O'Neil John, 1755
    John, Creechalaghta, 1804
O'Neill Cornelius, Lisnacoffery, Co. Westmeath, 1792
    Henry, Aghamore, Co. Lt., 1746
    John, Fardromin, (copy) signed Neill but O'Neill in original in Prerogative, 1724-5
    Michael, Carrickakillin, 1811
    Owen, Drimlagh, Co. Lt., 1745
O'Reilly Bernard, Tullygullin, Co. Cavan, 1841
    Bryan, Cortrasna, Co. Cavan, 1780
    Edmond, Bawn, 1849
    Edward, Tullygullen, Co. Cavan, 1834
    Mary, Dundavan, Co. Cavan, 1835
O'Reily Patrick (Rev., P.P.), Aughadrinan and Collumkill, 1833
Orr Robert, Torbuoy, Co. Lfd., 1808
O'Sullivan Patrick, Asnagh, Co. Lfd., 1808
Owens Bryan, Clommlegan, Co. Lt., 1844

A page from the
'Index to Ardagh Wills'
published as a supplement to the
'Irish Ancestor' journal, (Vol.III, No.2, 1971)

Wills from 1858 to the present

As one element of the disestablishment of the Church of Ireland, the 1857 Probate Act transferred testamentary jurisdiction to a new civil Court of Probate. A Principal Registry was set up in Dublin with eleven District Registries covering the rest of the country. The District Registry of Mullingar serves Westmeath.

Calendars of Wills and Administrations

Indices of Grants of probate and administration after 1858 are in the calendars of wills and administrations in the reading room of the NAI. They are indexed, one or two volumes per year, with a consolidated index for the period 1858-77. They give name, address, occupation and date of death and often the grantee's relationship to the deceased. When an entry of interest is identified in the calendars, the alphabetical testamentary card index must be consulted in order to establish if the actual document survives. Note that some documents which have survived may be fire-damaged and, pending conservation, unavailable for research.

CLEARY James [27a] 26 February Probate of the Will of **James Cleary** late of Cloghan Mullingar County **Westmeath** Farmer who died **12 January 1906** granted at **Mullingar** to Patrick Cleary Auctioneer Effects £4,140 16s. 6d.   (Former Grant 31 March 1906)

An entry from the *Calendar of grants of probate of wills and letters of administration* made in the Principal Registry and its district registries, 1923

Surviving Material of the Principal Registry

Source	Surviving Material in the NAI
Will Books	1874 (G-M); 1878 (A-Z); 1891 (G-M); 1896 (A-F)
Grants	1878; 1883; 1891; 1893.

Surviving Material of Mullingar District Registry

Source	Surviving Material in the NAI
Will Books	1858-1901

Other Collections and Indexes

Registry of Deeds

A sizeable number of deeds were registered in the Registry of Deeds in Dublin. Abstracts of Wills registered there during the period 1708 to 1842 have been published as *'Registry of Deeds, Dublin: Abstracts of Wills'*. in three volumes as follows:

Volume 1	1708 – 1745	ed. P.B. Eustace, (Dublin) 1954
Volume 2	1746 – 1785	ed. P.B. Eustace, (Dublin) 1956
Volume 3	1785 – 1832	ed. P.B. Eustace & E. Ellis (Dublin) 1984

---

44 PRICE, HERBERT, Mullingar, Co. Westmeath, Esq.
22 Dec. 1748. Full 1 p. 24 Jan. 1748/9.

To be privately buried at Mullingar. My sister Dudley Jervis. My grand-daughter Ann Ambrose. My grand-daughter Elinor Williamson. My son-in-law Anthony Lennon, exor. My son-in-law Henry Guyon. My daughter Sabina Lennon. My daughter Catherine Lennon. My daughter Margt. Guyon.([1]) Her two children by her first husband, viz. Jno. Wilson and Margaret Wilson, to have an equal share in a legacy with " her other children."

My leases from George Earl of Granard in the Manor of Mullingar. Rest of real and personal estate.

Witnesses: Stephen Bootle, Newtown, Co. Westmeath, clerk, Charles Coghlan, Mullingar, Doctor of Physick, Anthony Fearns.

Memorial witnessed by: Anthony Fearns, Mullingar, Doctor of Physick, John Saule, Dublin, gent.

133, 195, 90254   Anthony Lennon (seal)

An abstract from
Registry of Deeds, Dublin: Abstracts of Wills, Volune II.
- see above.

Genealogical Office
This office holds a sizeable collection of pre-1900 Irish Wills and abstracts. *'An Index of Will Abstracts in the Genealogical Office, Dublin'* compiled by P.B.Eustace was published in the Irish Manuscripts Commission's, *'The Genealogical Office, Dublin'* (Dublin) 1998. pp.79 – 282. The index was also published in Analecta Hibernica Vol.17, pp.151 – 348.

Land Commission
An index to the Wills held by the Land Commission is available in the NLI.

Copies and Abstracts of Irish Wills
A 'Guide to Copies and Abstracts of Irish Wills' by the Rev. Wallace Clare (Sharman 1930) is a valuable aid to the researcher, as it provides a single alphabetical index to the following collections:
- Copies and abstracts of Irish Wills deposited in the SOG
- Copies of Wills in all the Prerogative Will books which were salvaged from the PRO fire.
- Early original Wills deposited in English archives.
- Copies and abstracts of Wills published in some historical and genealogical journals, family histories etc.

The above guide is arranged as follows: name, address, date of probate and a key to one of the above.

Index of Irish Wills 1484 – 1858.
An 'Index of Irish Wills 1484 – 1858' provides a comprehensive index to the surviving testamentary records in the NAI. It also includes the Inland Revenue Will Registers and Administration Registers, 1829 – 1839. It is published on CD-Rom by Eneclann at www.eneclann.ie and on-line at www.findmypast.ie

Wills of Irish Soldiers 1914 – 1918
'World War I Irish Soldiers – Their Final Testament' is an index to the Wills of 9,000 Irish Soldiers who died during the conflict of 1914 – 1918, which were deposited in the NAI. It contains the soldier's name, rank, serial number, regiment, date of death, date the Will was written, war office number, war office data, record number and name of witnesses. It is published on CD-Rom by Eneclann at www.eneclann.ie

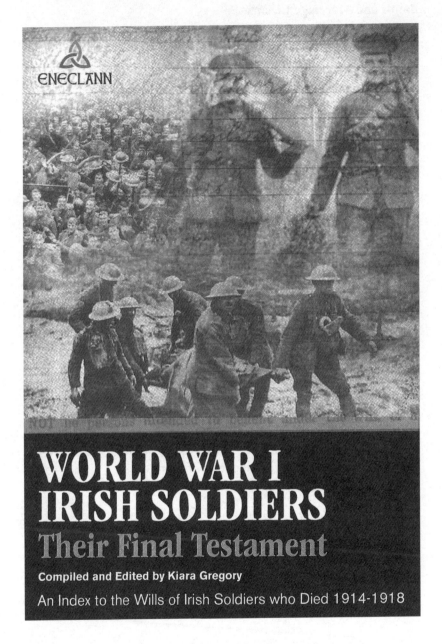

WORLD WAR I
IRISH SOLDIERS
Their Final Testament
Compiled and Edited by Kiara Gregory

An Index to the Wills of Irish Soldiers who Died 1914-1918

World War I Irish Soldiers - Thier Final Testament
published on CD from www.eneclann.ie
- see page 102.

Banns and Marriage Licences.

Churches had several methods to ensure that there was no impediment to a marriage. Banns required the intending couple to having their intentions read or posted three weeks in advance of the wedding date to allow for any objections to be made. Banns could be waived by payment of a fee to the Church of Ireland minister and this was the usual practice. Prior to 1858 the CoI required those wishing to obtain a licence to marry without having banns called to enter into a bond, i.e. a payment or surety to indemnify the church against damages that may be sought if there were objections raised later.

Indices to Marriage Licences Bonds in the NAI:
• Meath 1665, 1702 – 1845 WW43

Marriage Settlements

A marriage settlement was a type of deed and was a way of providing for a wife should her future husband find himself in financial difficulties. It was customary for a father to bestow a dowry upon his daughter at her marriage and as married women could not hold on to property in their own right the granting of the dowry to trustees provided some future security should the need arise. There were two types of settlement: a pre-marriage settlement and a post-marriage settlement, the information contained being similar to that found in a deed. Marriage settlements are found in family and estate collections, at the Registry of Deeds, NAI, NLI and sometimes in solicitor's offices.

Chapter 9   Newspapers

Irish newspapers have been published since the late 1600's, but the earliest for Westmeath date from the early nineteenth century. One major value lies in their news items and advertisements which give us an insight into the social and economic life of our ancestors. From the genealogist's point of view, the notices of births, deaths and marriages were usually for the better-off with the names of the poorer classes only appearing in reports of court cases, evictions and similar procedures. Towards the end of the nineteenth century and early twentieth century obituaries began to appear and this is of particular relevance to Catholics as place of burial is usually referred to and this detail is very rarely recorded anywhere else. At various times newspapers published names of those petitioning for a cause, those attending political meetings, contributing to various causes, and those applying for a vote or those entitled to vote. Transcripts from newspapers are to be found in the Moran Manuscripts (see Page 57) and Burgess papers (see page 58). Micheál Ó Conláin transcribed the records of Mullingar Town Commissioners from the newspapers. This can be consulted at WL. *Proceedings of Mullingar Town Commission 1856-1899,* Castlepollard, 2006, (typescript).

The Newsplan Report, which is the result of a co-operative initiative for Irish and UK newspapers, is available on www.nli.ie. The NLI, BL and WL hold newspapers relating to Westmeath on microfilm and some may be accessed by subscription at www.irishnewsarchive.com

UNITED IRISH LEAGUE

MEETING   BALLYMORE

On Sunday, at two o'clock, a most enthusiastic meeting was held at Ballymore, about twelve miles from Athlone, for the purpose of establishing a branch of the United Irish League in the district, and judging from the determination of those present, the near future will see a flourishing branch of the organisation in the locality. Mr John Greenan presided. Amongst those present were—Messrs Patrick Dooley, D C; John Cleary, John Greenan, Michael Delahunty, James Carney, Thomas Farrell, John M'Grath, Myles M'Grath, John Cashel, Pat Duragin, J Cleary, M Cormack, William Cormack, Hugh Rorke, John Dillon, William Brennan, John Carey, John O'Farrell, Christopher Macken, Thomas Slavin, Thomas Cormack, Thos Finn, Andrew Hayden, Owen Higgins, Patrick Clarke, Thomas Cunningham, James Downes, John M'Donnell, Thomas Dunnigan, Nicholas M'Grath, Thomas Dillon, James Ward, William Night, Joseph Lynam, Thomas Keenan, William M'Loughlin, James Ratigan, Michael Hyland, Patt Clarke, William Sheridan, Thomas Cunningham, John Finn, Peter Higgins, James Robinson, Owen Slaman, Peter M Lynam, Geo Knight, Peter Finn, William Sparks, Thomas Cormack, sen; Nicholas Cunningham, John Reynolds, Thomas Dwyer, Edwd Cormack, Wm Tarty, Thomas Mahon, Thomas Higgins, Patt Mahon, Patt Keenan, John Dillon, James Finn,

A news item from the *'Freeman's Journal'* on 14th November 1900

National newspapers such as the
'Irish Times' at www.irishtimes.com/search/
and 'The Freeman's Journal' at www.irishnewsarchive.com/
can also provide some valuable information of local interest.

The following is a list of newspapers published in Westmeath indicating where they are held. They are available on microfilm unless otherwise stated.

Athlone Conservative Advocative and Ballinasloe Reporter
Published: Athlone 1837
BL/NLI/WL Holdings: June - September 1837

Athlone Independent or Midland Telegraph
Published: Athlone 1833 – 1836
BL/NLI/WL Holdings: 6 Nov. 1833 – 9 Nov. 1836

Athlone Mirror, Westmeath and Roscommon Reformer
Published: Athlone 1841 – 1842
BL/NLI/WL Holdings: 18 Sept. 1841 – 16 July 1842

Athlone News
Published: Athlone 1961 – 1962
BL/NLI/WL Holdings: 2 Dec 1961 – 23 March 1962

Athlone Sentinel
Published: Athlone 1834 – 1861
BL/NLI/WL Holdings: 21 Nov. 1834 – 31 July 1861

Athlone Times
Published: Athlone 1877 – 1902
BL Holdings: May 1899 – Jan 1902
NLI Holdings: 19-26 Nov 1887; 1899. 4 May 1889 – 25 Jan 1902
WL Holdings: 19-26 Nov 1887; 4 May 1889 – 25 Jan 1902

Midland Chronicle and Westmeath Independent
Published: Mullingar 1827 – 1827
BL/NLI/WL Holdings: 10 Jan. – 7 Nov. 1827

Midland Herald
Published: Mullingar ca.1947 – 1957
NLI/WL Holdings: 6 Jan 1949 – 1956; 6 Jan. 1949 – 17 Jan. 1957
Hardcopy.

Midland Reporter and Westmeath Nationalist
See Westmeath Nationalist and Midland Reporter.

Topic
Published: Mullingar 1971 (began as *Topic* (1971-ca.1975), *Midland Topic* (ca.1975-1989) *Westmeath Topic* 1989 – to date.
BL Holdings: 1989 – to date
NLI Holdings: 1989 – 2005
WL Holdings: 1975-77, 1986 – to date (Hardcopy)

Westmeath Examiner
Published: Mullingar 1882 – to date. Also published an Athlone edition Oct 1974 – Nov 1979, which became the Athlone Examiner 1 Dec 1979 – 12 Jan. 1991.
BL/WL Holdings: 23 Sept 1882 – to date
NLI Holdings: 23 Sept 1882 – 30 Sept 1905; 1906 – 1985; 1989 – 1997; 1999 - to date
www.irishnewsarchives.com Holdings: 1882 – to date

Westmeath Guardian
Published: Mullingar 1835 – 1928
BL / NLI Holdings: 8 Jan 1835 – 19 Oct 1928
WL Holdings: 8 Jan 1835 – 1896

Westmeath Herald and General Advertiser
Published: Athlone 30 Apr 1859 – 28 Apr 1860
BL Holdings: 30 Apr 1859 – 28 Apr 1860
WL Holdings: 1859 – 1860

Westmeath Independent
Published: Athlone 13 June 1846 – July 1968. Not published 30 Oct 1920 – 4 Feb 1922. Amalgamated with *Offaly Independent* and continued as *Westmeath Offaly Independent* Aug 1968 – 17 May 1985
BL Holdings: 13 June 1846 – 14 Aug 1880; 25 Sept., 2, 16 Oct. 1880 – 26 Mar., 6, 13 Aug. 1881; 12 Nov 1881 – 10 Feb., 7 Apr., 10 Nov. 1883; 16 Feb. 1884 – 30 Oct. 1920; 4 Feb. 1922 –
NLI Holdings: 13 June 1846 - 1896; 1897 – 1905, 1906 – 1920, 1920; 1923 - 1985, 1986 – 2006, 2007 -
WL Holdings: 1860 – 1920, 1923 – to-date

(courtesy of Westmeath Examiner)

Collinstown Parish

Rev. L. Farreily, P P, - -	£1.	0	0
Rev. D Cuskelly CC - -	1.	0	0
Messrs. Edward Cantwell, PLG	1.	0	0
" Patrick Daly - -	1.	0	0
" William McCormick -	1.	0	0
" Robert McCormick - -	1.	0	0
" Christopher Lavey - -	1.	0	0
" Francis Adlum - -	1.	0	0
Mrs. Salmon - -	0	10	0
Messrs. John Ryan - -	0	10	0
" Charles McDermott - -	0.	10	0
" Richard Shaw - -	0	5	0
" Andrew Coffey - -	0	5	0
" Michael Rock - -	0	5	0
" Laurence Carley - -	0	5	0
" Joseph Fagan - -	0	5	0
" Patrick Cole PLG - -	0	5	0
" Thomas Fagan - -	0	4	0

The following 3s each – Bartle Fagan, William Weeds, Christopher Lestrange.

The following 2s 6d each – Owen Weir, Mrs M. Daly, Richard Riggs, Pat Bray, James McGennis, Michael Murphy, John Weir, Mrs Tormey, John Magrath, Mrs Broughan, John Mangan, John Ward.

2s each: - Mrs Martin, Pat Garry, John Doyne, Pat Gilsenan, Mat Kennedy, James Murray, Pat Cahill, Thomas Salmon, Michael Smyth (Labourer), Michael Heffernan, James Gibney, William Maguire, William Fogan, A Friend.

1s. each: - Pat Foley, John Foley, John Macken, Pat Murray, Dan Gegan, Pat Dalton, Christopher Coleman, Michael Rock, Ned Godfrey, Pat Lynch, Mrs McDonnell, James Tuite, Thomas Smyth, William Mulvany, Pat Hannon, John McDonnell, Mrs Weldon, James

A list of subscribers from Collinstown Parish published in the *Westmeath Examiner* on 13th May 1883.

Westmeath Journal
Published: Mullingar 1812 – 1834
BL and WL Holdings: 27 May 1813, 2 Jan 1823 – 19 Oct 1834
NLI Holdings: 1823 – 1 May 1834

Westmeath Nationalist and Midland Reporter
30 April 1891-16 Sept. 1897 contd. as Midland Reporter and Westmeath Nationalist 23 Sept. 1897 – 21 Sept. 1939
Published: Mullingar 1891-1939
BL Holdings: 30 April – 1891 – 1928; Jan. 1931 – 21 Sept. 1939
NLI Holdings: 13 April 1891 – 1920; Aug 1927 – 1939
WL Holdings: 13 April 1891 – 16 Sept. 1897

Newspaper adverts can also provide a range
of useful information to the researcher

Chapter 10   Directories and Occupational Sources

Directories are guides to traders, professions and gentry in particular areas. These were privately produced and are an excellent genealogical source for traders, professionals and public officials. However, some are very limited in scope, e.g. *The Post-chaise Companion,* 1784 gives names of noblemen and gentlemen only. The guides were commercial ventures published by a few prominent companies, such as Pigot and Slater. Most began publishing in the 1820s and they gradually expanded the numbers of towns included, and also the extent of coverage within each town. They will typically list names in alphabetical order under the headings: nobility, gentry and clergy, professional persons, academics and schools, hotels, shopkeepers and traders, places of worship and public institutions. A check through the different years will show when a name ceases to be mentioned – hence an ancestor may have moved out of an area or died. It is important to remember that the reliability of these directories may be questionable; therefore they should only be used as a general guide. They are available in major Irish-interest libraries and also on CD from Eneclann www.eneclann.ie, and some are on-line at http://failteromhat.com/pigot.htm and www.findmypast.ie The Directories for Westmeath are listed below and the towns covered are shown in the table.

Leet, Ambrose, *An alphabetical list of noted places, market towns, villages, gentlemen's seats, townlands and signal stations in Ireland etc.,* 2 vols., Dublin, 1812; also a 2nd ed., Dublin, 1814.

Pigot's Commercial Directory of Ireland, 1824. Includes Athlone, Ballymore, Castletowndelvin, Kilbeggan, Kinnegad and Mullingar.

TALLOW CHANDLERS.
Kergan Elizabeth, Main-st
Nowlan Richd. Main-st
Tuite Thos. Main-st

TANNERS.
Keena Pat. Main-st
Mc Cornice Thos. Main-st
Tuite Thos. Main-st

WATCH & CLOCK-MAKERS
Barber Wm. Main-st
Brock Aunger, Main-st
Murphy Andrew, Main-st

WINE MERCHANTS
Delany Robt. Main-st
Kenny Timothy, Main-st
Mahon Morth, Main-st
Peacy Geo. Main-st
Salmon Jas. Main-st

Miscellaneous.
Conoly Patrick, druggist, Main-st

An extract of merchants in Mullingar from
Pigot's Commercial Directory of 1824
- see above.

Slater, I., *National Commercial Directory of Ireland, 1846.*
Includes Athlone, Castlepollard, Kilbeggan and Ballinagore, Kinnegad,
Mullingar.

Slater, I., *National Commercial Directory of Ireland 1856.* Includes
Athlone, Castlepollard, Castletowndelvin, Kilbeggan and Ballinagore,
Kinnegad, Moate, Mullingar, Tyrell's Pass.

NOBILITY, GENTRY AND CLERGY.

Adams Francis, Esq. Rathconnell Castle   [brook
Barlow Robt. Esq. M.D. & J.P. Anne-
Browne Hon. and Rev. Henry Montague, the Glebe
Cantwell Right Rev. John, D.D. and R. C. Bishop of Meath, Chapel House
Caulfield Colonel John, Bloomfield
CookeAdolphus,Esq.Cookesborough
De Blaquiere John, Esq. Portlemon
Dunn Rev. Robert H., Churchtown Glebe   [Carrick
Featherston H. William, Esq. J. P.
Featherston H. William, Esq. jun. Robinstown   [derry
Fitzgerald William, Esq. Ballin-
Fleming James, Esq. Boardstown
Frazer Lieutenant Thomas Wallace (pensioners' staff), Church st
French Arthur, Esq. R.M. Lamancha
Geoghegan Rev.Edward, Mill Mount
Gibbons James, Esq. Ballinagall
Gibson Rev. Alexander, Main st
Hall Rev. Boud, Taghmon   [Glebe
Hickey Rev. Noah S., Portnashangan
Hopkins Sir Francis, Bart. J.P. Rochford House
Joly Charles, Esq. Clonmoyle
Kelly John H. Esq. Charleville
Kilmaine Right Hon. Lord, Gaulstown Park
L'Estrange Francis, Esq. Keoltown
L'Estrange Torianno, Esq. J.F. Lynn
Levinge Chas. Esq. Levington Park
Levinge Godfrey, Esq. J. P. Culliau
Levinge Hugh, Esq. Clan Hugh
Levinge Marcus Anthony, Esquire, Charlestown   [Enniscoffey
Levinge Marcus Anthony, jun. Esq.
Levinge Sir Richard, Bart. D.L. & J.P. Knockdrin Castle
Levinge Richd. H. Esq. J. P. Levington Park
Levinge Wm. Esq. Knockdrin Castle
Lyons John Chas. Esq. J.P. Ladiston

Martin Bernard, Esq. Main st
Martin Rev. Robt. Moyliscar Rectory
Matthews Mrs. Mary Ann, Main st
Murphy Patrick, E. J.P. Ballinacloon
MurrayHenry,Esq.J.P.MountMurray
Nugent Sir Percy, Bart. J. P. Donore
Reilly William, Esq. J. P. Bellmont
Rennell Richd. W. Esq. J.P. Killynon
Robinson William, Anneville
Sheil John H. Esq. J.P. Gortumloe
Smith Francis P. Esq. J.P. Larkfield
Smyth Robert, Esq. J.P. Gaybrook
Swift Richard, Esq. J.P. Portwilliam
Tuite Hugh Morgan, Esq. M. P. and J. P. Lonna House
Uniacke Thomas Fane, Esq. Lynnberry House
Walsh Thomas, Esq. Bellevue

ACADEMIES AND SCHOOLS.

DIOCESAN SCHOOL, Mill mount— Rev. Edward Geoghan, master
Hogan John, Harbour st
NATIONAL SCHOOL (boys') Church street—Peter Cribbens, master
NUNS' SCHOOL (girls') the Nunnery, the ladies of the convent, teachers
PROTESTANT FREE SCHOOL, Longford road—Wm. Speight, master

APOTHECARIES.

Kelly Dillon, Main st
Kiernan Owen, Main st
Middleton Laurence, Main st

ATTORNEYS.

Fitzgerald John, Main st
Gunning George Robert, Chapel lane
Stanley Edmund, Main st
Tilson William, Main st
Walsh Thomas, Bellevue

AUCTIONEERS.

Hanlon Michael, Gaol st
Lee Warren (and commissioner of affidavits), Main street

BAKERS.

Canton Mary, Main st
Carey James, Main st   [Main st
Downes Joseph (and confectioner),
Farrell Patrick, Main st
Halican Joseph, Gaol st

74

A page from
Slater's National Commercial Directory of Ireland, 1846.

Slater, I., *National Commercial Directory of Ireland, 1870.* Includes Athlone, Castlepollard, Castletown-Delvin, Kilbeggan, Kinnegad, Moate, Mullingar.

Slater, I., *National Commercial Directory of Ireland, 1881.* Includes Athlone, CastlePollard, Castletown-Delvin, Kilbeggan and Tyrrell's Pass, Moate, Mullingar.

Slater, I., *National Commercial Directory of Ireland 1894.* (Coverage as above).

Stokes, G.T., Burgess, John, Editor, *Athlone, the Shannon and Lough Ree, with a local directory,* Dublin, 1897.

[W. Wilson], *The Post-chaise Companion: or, Traveller's Directory through Ireland,* Dublin, 1784.

See also Burgess Papers on page 58.

GENTRY & CLERGY.

Campbell Henry, Esq. Halston, Bally-more
Clibborn Mrs. Isabella, Moate
Clibborn William C. Esq. Moate View
Daly Arthur C. Esq. Moate
Digby Captain William Benjamin, Ballincur, Ballymore
Egan William, Esq. Moate Lodge
Fairbrother Adam, Esq. Farnagh
Fetherston H. James, Esq. J.P. Ballintubber
Fetherston H. Theobald, Esq. Moate
Fetherston H. William, Esq. J.P. Grouse Lodge
Fosbery Captain Wydenham, Moate
French Digby, Esq. Moate
Fry Alexander, Esq. Moate

An extract of Gentry and Clergy in Moate
from *Slater's 1881 Directory* - see above.

COUNTY GAOL, MULLINGAR.

Board of Superintendence, Sir Percy Nugent, bart.; John Charles Lyons, esq.; William Fetherston H., esq.; Richard W. Reynell, esq.; William Adams Reilly, esq.; Thomas F. Uniacke, esq.; Francis P. Smythe, esq.; Richard Swift, esq.; John Caulfield, esq.; Godfrey Levinge, esq.; Henry Murray, esq.; Cuthbert J. Clibborn, esq.; Charles Arabin, esq.
Inspector and Chaplain, Hon. and Rev. Henry M. Browne.
R. C. Chaplain, Rev. James Savage.
Presbyterian Chaplain, Rev. Alexander Gibson.
Surgeon, Joseph Ferguson, M.D.
Apothecary, Laurence Middleton, esq.
Governor, James Tyrrell, esq.

BRIDEWELL AND KEEPER.
Moate, Daniel Lewis.

COUNTY INFIRMARY, MULLINGAR.
Surgeon, Joseph Ferguson, M.D.

DISTRICT LUNATIC ASYLUM AT MARYBOROUGH.
Manager, William Abbott, esq.
Physician, Dr. Jacob.

MEDICAL OFFICER OF FEVER HOSPITAL.
Castlepollard, D. H. MacAdam, M.D.

MEDICAL OFFICERS OF DISPENSARIES.
Athlone, G. Hetherington, M.B.
Ballinacargy, J. F. West, M.D.
Balnalack, G. Pallas, M.D.
Castlepollard, D. H. MacAdam, M.D.
Castletowndelvin, J. W. Williams, M.B.
Clonmellon, Henry Davidge.
Collinstown, G. M. Davidge.
Drumcree, M. T. Gallagher, M.R.C.S.L.
Glasson, E. James Fallon, L.R.C.S.I.
Kilbeggan, S. A. Duigan, M.R.C.S.L.
Killucan, R. R. Cornwall, M.D.
Kinnegad, Joseph Lightburne.
Knockdrin and Monilea, Gabriel Stokes, M.D.
Milltown, John G. Battersby, M.D.

An extract of public officials from the 1847
edition of *Thom's Directory*
- see below.

Thom's Directories

From 1844 the publisher, Alexander Thom, produced an annual national directory. It covers residents, traders, merchants and includes various lists of officials. Some of the earlier editions provide a brief historical and social background to the larger towns and villages. It is available in most libraries in hard copy and on microfilm. Some years are available on CD from www.eneclann.ie and www.findmypast.ie

Occupational Sources

The following is a list of some helpful sources listing persons with particular occupations:

Authors: Keaney, Marian, *Westmeath Authors: a bibliographical and biographical study, Mullingar,* 1969.

Education: Records of teachers can be found in the NAI. A card index divided into counties in the reading room guides one to the records sought (See Chapter 12).

Medical Profession: *Medical directory for Ireland,* London, 1852. Archive CD Books Ireland, 2005.

UK Medical Registers: The Registers for 1859 to 1959 for all of Great Britain and Ireland, are available for online searching at the subscription site www.ancestry.co.uk The information for each registrant is: date of registration, name, address, qualifications and dates awarded. The Registers were updated every few years, so that examination of later Registers will reveal changes of address and will even indicate the approximate year of death (disappearance of the entry).

Military Service: Thousands of Irishmen served in the British Army, and their records are held in the National Archives, Kew www.nationalarchives.gov.uk and are classed as War Office (WO) Records. These records commenced prior to most parish records and are rich in detail. They can be divided into a number of categories:-

1760–1920 British Army service records: These are available for inspection in UK National Archives in Kew. The early records show; name, parish of birth; age, date and place of enlistment; locations and dates of service; rank(s); comments on conduct; date and reason for discharge; age and physical description on discharge; intended place of residence following discharge; trade or occupation. Records from the 1850s will also show the name and address of next of kin; date and place of the marriage is often given.

The records from 1760 to 1913, which pertain only to personnel who were discharged on pension, are available for online searching at the subscription site www.findmypast.co.uk. First World War service records, 1914/1920, including records of personnel who died during service, (as well as those discharged on pension), are available for online searching at the subscription site www.ancestry.co.uk.

Unfortunately, about 60% of the records of those who served during the First World War, including the records of those who were discharged prior to the War and later re-enlisted, were destroyed in an air raid in July 1940.

Note that Irish Catholics were prohibited from bearing arms until 1793. However Catholics were recruited, for service abroad only, from 1756. Catholics joined the Army in increasing numbers from that time. *A Guide to Irish Military Heritage* by Brian Hanley (Four Courts Press 2004) is an excellent guide to those researching Irish military history, and see also Bureau of Military history at www.bureauofmilitaryhistory.ie/

Millers: *The Millers and the Mills of Ireland of about 1850: a list* by William E. Hogg, 2nd edition, Dublin, 2000. Micheál Ó Conláin , Editor, *A provisional list of mills of County Westmeath*, Castlepollard, 2005. (typescript). WL.

Royal Irish Constabulary: (RIC) members. The records of all 90,000 members of the RIC are in the Public Record Office in London (Ref. HO 184.43). A copy (Ref. MFA 24/1-16) is in NAI. The records are indexed by initial letter of the surname in two periods i.e. 1816-67 and 1867-1922. The information includes age and date of entry; height; religion, native county; trade; marital status; county of wife; postings; promotions and punishments and dates of same. The Index to these records is available for online searching at the subscription site www. ancestry.co.uk. Jim Herlihy,*The Royal Irish Constabulary; A Complete Alphabetical List of Officers and Men, 1816-1922,* Dublin, 1999, provides a reference number for every name listed. Also Jim Herlihy, *The Royal Irish Constabulary; A Short History and Genealogical Guide,* Dublin, 2000.

Postal Service Appointment Books: These books, dating from 1737, are available for searching at the subscription site www.ancestry.co.uk For each person appointed, the following details are recorded:- Name and date of appointment, title of position (eg Postman, Rural Postman, Clerk), post office to which assigned.

Religious: Irish Catholic Directory: clerical obituaries, ordination lists, register of ecclesiastical events, 1836-1975. NLI, P. 7624-7628.

Condon, Kevin, *The Missionary College of All Hallows 1842-1891*, Dublin, 1986. (contains a list of students/ordinations)

Hamell, Patrick J. and Ó Fiaich, Tomás, *Maynooth Students and Ordinations index 1795-1895*, Birr, 1982.

Hamell, Patrick J., *Maynooth Students and Ordinations 1895-1984*, Birr, 1984.

The following titles include information on clergy who served in the different parishes and clergy who were born in the different parishes in the diocese of Meath: (Cogan's *Diocese of Meath* is also available on line at www.askaboutireland.ie)

Cogan, A., *The Diocese of Meath ancient and modern*, Vol. I, Dublin, 1862; Vol. II, Dublin, 1867; Vol. III, Dublin, 1870.

Curran, Olive C., *History of the Diocese of Meath 1860-1993, 3 vols.*, Mullingar, 1995. (includes index of Priests from the 1700s by Rev. Paul Connell).

Dunne, Daniel, Editor, *The Town at the crossroads, Baile na gCros, a History of Castlepollard, Castletown and Finea parish,* [Castlepollard], [2007].

O'Brien, Gearoid, *St. Mary's Parish, Athlone: a history*, Longford, 1989. This work has biographical notes on priests who served in the parish, or who were native to the parish.

Chapter 11 — Memorial Inscriptions

Gravestone inscriptions, wall plaques in churches, names inscribed on stained glass windows and name plates on seats are all forms of memorial inscription. Their limitations include the fact that not all families were in a position to fund such memorials, and that headstone inscriptions may be illegible due to damage or weather. In addition the inscription may not always be correct. However, the information given on such memorials may never be found anywhere else and usually includes dates, places of residence and relationships of the deceased. For an excellent account of the history of burial grounds see James G. Ryan's *Irish Church Records* (Flyleaf Press, 2001). One must always check CoI burial grounds for all denominations. Catholic headstones may be evident in CoI graveyards as they usually bear the inscription 'I H S'. The stonemason's name may be engraved on the gravestone and a little research on this name may well provide a date when the stone was erected. Old and disused graveyards must be approached with great care both out of respect for the dead and for your own safety. Overgrowth should be gently removed and nothing only plain water and a clean paint brush should be used to try to read the inscription.

Surveys of Westmeath graveyards by local community groups and individuals are available as published works and on the internet. Others are available in typescript format in Westmeath Library. Below is an alphabetical list of surveyed graveyards indicating the Civil Parish in which each is located. The three main sources referenced are:

JAPMDI; *Journal of the Association for the Preservation of the Memorials of the Dead, Ireland* (continued as *Journal of The Irish Memorials Association*, 1892 – 1934).

MWC1; M. Ó Conláin. A Partial List of Memorials in Westmeath Churchyards (WL)

MWC2; M. Ó Conláin. Inscriptions in Westmeath Churchyards, Part 2. (WL)

Graveyard (Civil Parish) Location of Record

Almoritia (Ballymorin) JAPMDI 2 Pp.556; 7, pp.680-682; MWC2 Pp.s 2 - 21, (typescript), WL.

Archerstown (Castletowndelvin) MWC1, pp.187-202, (typescript), (WL).

Ardnacraney (Noughaval) JAPMDI, 4, p.489.

Ardnurcher (Ardnurcher or Horseleap) JAPMDI, 6, pp.608-609; 7, pp.121, 191; 8, pp.642-644; 9, pp.170-173; 11, pp.236-237, 332-333; MWC1, pp.2 – 11.

Athlone Abbey Franciscan Graveyard (St. Mary's) Hazel J. Ryan, Athlone Abbey Graveyard, Mullingar, 1987, (HR). JAPMDI, 4, pp.493-494, 5, pp.481-484; 6, pp.160-162; 11, pp 333-335.

Athlone St. Mary's (St. Mary's) JAPMDI, 2, pp.227-232, 374-388, 557-561; 3, pp.170-173, 346-349, 521-523; 4, pp.135-137; 5, pp.272, 485; 6, pp.162-163. NLI p.5309, Burgess Papers (BP), see p.x: J.S. Jolly, 1896, Marsh's Library, Ms. Z3.3.1

Athlone St. Mary's Church of Ireland (St. Mary's) Liz FitzPatrick, An account of the graveyard and gravestone inscriptions of St. Mary's Church of Ireland, Athlone, Co. Westmeath, (typescript), (WL).

Athlone St. Peter's (St. Peter's). JAPMDI, 4, p.486. NLI p.5309, BP.

Ballinacor Bridge (Castletowndelvin) JAPMDI, 1, p.245; 2, p.174; 3, p.523.

Balrath (Castletownkindalen) MWC2, p.281.

Balreadh (Rathconnell) MWC1, pp.622-627.

Ballyglass (Mullingar) Register of Internments in Ballyglass Cemetery 24.03.1891-03.03.1911.Microfilm (Mf), (WL).

Ballyloughloe (Ballyloughloe) JAPMDI, 3, p.523; 11, pp.237-240 & pp.335-336: 12, pp.124-125; MWC1, pp.12-16 & 356-357. Irish Ancestor (2) 1972, pp.105-112.

Ballymorin (Ballymorin) See Almoritia.

Ballymore (Ballymore) JAPMDI, 8, pp.443-448; Jeremiah Sheehan, Ed., Beneath the Shadow of Uisneach: Ballymore & Boher, (Ballymore), 1996; pp.421-464, (JS); MWC1, pp.17-22.

Boher (Kilcleagh (2)) JS, pp.474-484.

Boherquill (Streete) MWC1, pp.611-621.

Bunowen (Bunowen) JAPMDI, 4, pp.489-490. BP; MWC1, p.23.

Carrick (Carrick) JAPMDI, 9, pp.555-556; MWC1, pp.24-25.

Castlelost (Castlelost) JAPMDI, 9, pp.382-384; MWC, pp.26-28.

Castlepollard (Rathgarve) JAPMDI, 4, pp.486, 494-497; 5, p.274.

Castletown- Geoghegan (Castletownkindalen) JAPMDI, 1, pp.513-514; 2, pp.371-373; 4, p.490; 6, pp.163-614; MWC1, pp.37-47.

Cathedral Grounds (Mullingar) MWC2, p.61.

Churchtown (Churchtown) MWC2, pp.336-345.

Churchtown (Rathconrath) MWC2, pp.314 – 327.

Clonarney (Clonarney) MWC1, pp.203-213.

Clonfad (Killucan (2)) JAPMDI, 10, p.247; MWC1, pp.75-79.

Clonkeen (Noughaval) MWC2, p.352.

Clonlost (Rathconnell) JAPMDI, 1, p.245; 11, pp.476-478; 12, pp.558-561; MWC1, pp.94-97.

Clonmellon (Killua) MWC1, pp.59-65.

Collinstown (St. Feighin's) JAPMDI, 5, p.273; MWC1, pp.98-99. MWC2, pp.390 – 395,

Coolamber(Street) JAPMDI, 10, p.247; MWC1, pp 528-569.

Coosan (St. Mary's) Register of interments 1968-2005, Mf., (WL).

Cornamagh (St. Mary's) Register of interments 1871-2005, Mf, (WL). (inc. name, address, age, marital status, occupation, date of death, person who paid for the interment, plot number. 1871-1901 NLI p.5309, BP.

Coralstown (Killucan) MWC2, pp.176 – 181.

Crowenstown (Castletowndelvin) MWC1, pp.214-228.

Delvin (Castletowndelvin) JAPMDI, 7, pp.682; MWC1, pp.159-184; Dr. Beryl F.E. Moore and Michael Kenny, *'Headstones in St. Mary's Churchyard, Delvin, Co. Westmeath, 1980'*, (BM), in Ir. Anc. 14 (1) (1982): pp., 39-57. WL.

Drumcree (Kilcumny) JAPMDI, 5, pp.112-114; MWC1, pp.235-240.

Drumraney (Drumraney) JAPMDI, 4, pp.489; 12, pp, 122-123, 561-562; MWC1, pp.241-243, MWC2, p.353,

Dunboden (Moylisker) MWC1, p.380.

Dysart (Dysart) MWC1, p.66.

Enniscoffey (Enniscoffey) MWC2, pp.183 – 201

Forgney (Piercetown) MWC1, pp.280-281.

Fore (St. Feighin's) JAPMDI, 1, pp.508-511; 2, pp.373-374; 4,pp.133-134 and 486-487; 6, p.410; MWC1, pp.100-158.

Gaulstown (Castlelost) MWC1, pp.29-36,

Griffinstown (Killucan) MWC1, pp.80-92.

Hopestown (Mullingar) MWC2, pp.64 – 68.

Kenny (Mullingar) MWC1, p.393; MWC2, pp.282 – 288.

Kilbeggan (Kilbeggan) JAPMDI, 7, pp.191-192; 11, p.336; MWC1, p.244. MWC2 pp.71 – 95.

Kilbixy (Kilbixy) JAPMDI, 5, pp.114-119; 12, p.124; MWC1, pp.254-270; Westmeath Genealogical Project, (WL)

Kilbreeda (Mullingar) MWC1, pp.382-383.

Kilbride (Moylisker) JAPMDI, 9, pp.556-557. MWC1 p.282-284.

Row 12

CLEMENTS. Domed headstone with full sunburst encircling a cross, IHS and heart, a flowering plant on each side. "Oh Lord have mercy on the soul of Catharine Clements (alias Seery) who depd this life Jan. 27 1807 (or 3) aged 49 years." At bottom "This Monut was erd by Patt Clements son Thos in Memory of her."

GLINNAN. This stone is broken in half and the following words are on the lower half. ". . . . Glinnan in memory . . . . Father Michael Glinnan who departed this life May the . . . . 1776 aged 63 Yrs. Of his Mother Elizabeth Glinnan who died May 25 1750 aged 61 Yrs."

LYNCH. Domed stone with sunburst, cross, IHS and heart with a plant in centre, a winged cherub's head on each side. "This monument was erected by Thomas John Patrick and Michael Lynch as a tribute of respect to the memory of their father Hugh Lynch who departed this life the 23rd of March 1799 aged 51 years. Also their Mother Catherine Lynch alias Quinn who departed this life the 25th of June 1798 aged 41 years."

Row 13

BURKE. Domed stone with full sunburst surrounding a cross, IHS and heart, leafy branch on each side and further out a dove with an olive branch, all surrounded by a lozenge border. Stone is leaning to the left and only some of the inscription can be read. "This stone was erected by James Burke in memory of his father Francis Burke who departed this life the 29th Novr 1809 aged 75 years . . . . May the souls of the faithful departed through the mercy of God rest in peace Amen."

BRAY. A yew tree growing beside this stone is forcing it forward. It is a solid cross with IHS in its centre. "Erected by Maurice Bray of Ballyhealy in memory of his beloved brother Patrick Bray who died September the 6th 1849 aged 22 years. Also his father Andrew Bray died January the 6th 1850 aged 60 years. And also his mother Anne Bray died October the 1st 1853 aged 54 years. And his Aunt Anne Bray died October the 3rd 1858 aged 62 years. His niece Anne Bray died January the 18th 1866 aged 7 years and also his brother Michael Bray died April the 4th 1875 aged 40 years." At bottom "May they rest in peace Amen."

HEGARTY. Stone leaning forward; domed top and *Gloria etc.* around the dome. "Erected by Jane Hegarty in memory of her beloved husband Maurice Hegarty of Belnaslea who died 15th April 1859 aged 44 years."

WARD. Stone broken into two diagonally, the bottom half lying here on the ground while the top half is lying on the ground at the end of the row. Part of the inscription is on each stone. "This stone was erected by Patrick Ward over his wife Honour Ward alias Dowlan who departed May 22nd 1741 aged 47 years. Memento Mori. Pray for the soul of Patrick Ward who erected this monument and departed this life October the 11th 1758 aged 69 years."

Entries from
'Headstones in St Mary's Churchyard, Delvin' published in the
Irish Ancestor Vol.14 (1) 1982, pp 39-57.

Kilcleagh (Kilcleagh) Liam Cox, Moate County Westmeath; a history of the town and district, Athlone, 1981; (LC), pp.232-233.

Kilcolumb (Killucan) MWC1, pp.67-69.

Kilcumney (Kilcumney) JAPMDI, 5, p.114; MWC1, pp.285-294

Kilcumreragh (Kilcumreragh) Jimmy Murray and Jeremiah Sheehan, *Rosemount Churches Past and Present*, Moate, 1995, (JM), pp.86-205; JAPMDI,8, pp.637–641; MWC1, pp.295-299.

Kilkenna (Killulagh) MWC1, pp.185-186.

Kilkenny West(KilkennyWest) JAPMDI 4, p.490; 12, pp.314, 434-435; MWC1 p.300, BP.

Killadoran (Castletowndelvin) MWC1, pp.229-234.

Killare (Killare) JAPMDI, 8, pp.180-181; 12, p.562. MWC1, pp.301-303. JS, pp.467-474.

Killaugh (Castletowndelvin) JAPMDI, 1, p.244. MWC1, p.304.

Killomenaghan (Kilcleagh) LC, pp.233-234.

Killua (Killua) MWC1, pp.48-58. Killua, Noel E. French (typescript), WL.

Killucan, St. Etchen's (Killucan) MWC2, pp.96-166, (typescript), (WL)

Killucan Presbyterian Church MWC2, pp.167-168, (typescript), (WL).

Killulagh (Castletowndelvin) JAPMDI, 1, p.245; 2, p.374: 7, pp.192,682-683. See also St. Mulchan's; MWC1,pp.305-319.

Kilmacnevan (Kilmacnevan) MWC1, pp.273-275. MWC2, pp.295-323.

Kilmaglish (Tyfarnham) MWC1, pp.628-630. MWC2, p.219.

Kinnegad (Killucan) MWC2, pp.172-175.

Kilpatrick (Kilpatrick) JAPMDI, 11, p.337. MWC1, pp.320-323.

Kilronan (Lynn) MWC1, pp.384-392. MWC2, pp.30-60.

Knockmant (Killucan) MWC1, pp.70-71.

Lacken (Multyfarnham) JAPMDI, 12, pp.314-317; Peter Wallace, Multyfarnham Parish History, Multyfarnham, 1984, (PW), p.197. MWC1, pp.324-336.

Leney (Lackan) JAPMDI, 11, p.337; MWC1, pp.337-339; MWC2, pp.247-276. PW, pp.197-201.

Lickblea (Lickbla) JAPMDI, 12, p.563.

Loughnavally (Churchtown) MWC2, p.346.

Lynn (Lynn) JAPMDI, 5, pp.486-489. MWC1, pp.370-373. Westmeath Genealogical Project, (WGP), (typescript), (WL).

Marlinstown (Mullingar) MWC2, pp.24-29.

Mayne (Mayne) JAPMDI, 5, p.119-120. Micheál Ó Conláin, Cemetery Records for Mayne and Faughalstown, (typescript), (WL)

Milltown (Rathconrath) MWC2, p.328.

Moate Church and Graveyard (Kilcleagh) JAPMDI, 11, pp.478-483; MWC1, pp.346-353; L.C., pp.231-232.

Moate, The Friends' Burial Ground, (Kilcleagh) JAPMDI, 11, pp.337-338; MWC1, pp.354-355. L.C., 230; Cox, L., Sheehan, J. and Tinsley,B., Moate Quaker Cemetery, Occasional Paper, No. 2, 1985,(typescript), (WL).

Mount Dalton Obelisk (Rathconrath) JAPMDI, 4, p.491.

Mount Temple aka Ballyloughloe (Ballyloughloe) See Ballyloughloe above.

Moyliscar (Moylisker) JAPMDI, 9, pp.557; MWC1,pp.374-379.

Moyvoughley Old School (Ballymore) MWC2, p.22.

Mullingar (Mullingar) JAPMDI, 9, pp.385-389; 10, pp.248; 11, pp.339-344.

Mullingar Presbyterian (Mullingar) MWC1, pp.368 and 394. MWC2, p.169.

MullingarAll Saints (Mullingar) MWC1, pp.358-367; MWC2, pp.214-118. WGP.

Mullingar Famine Graveyard (Mullingar) MCW2, p.23.

Mullingar Presentation Convent (Mullingar) MWC2, pp.62-63.

Multifarnham or Multyfanham (Multyfarnham) JAPMDI, 1, p.245, 512-513; MWC1, pp.340-5; MWC2, pp.245 & 278-280; PW, pp.201-202. See also Lacken.

Multifernan (sic) (Multyfarnham) JAPMDI, 2, pp.232-233; 4, pp.488-489.

Multifarnham Abbey (Multyfarnham) JAPMDI, 7, p.476; 10, pp 140-143; PW, pp.203-208; Pádraig Ó Gibealláin, Multyfarnham Abbey; Monuments and Memories, Multyfarnham, 1984.

Newtown Fertullagh JAPMDI, 3, pp.524-526; MWC1, pp.395-413.

Newtownlow (Newtown) Kathleen Flynn, Newtownlow, (typescript), (WL). MWC2, pp.396-405.

Noughaval [Noughaville] (Noughaval) JAPMDI, 12, pp.317-319; 4, p.489; MWC1, pp.414-415.

Pass of Kilbride (Pass of Kilbride) MWC2, pp.202-208.

Portloman (Portloman) MWC1, pp.416-421.

Portnashangan (Portnashangan) MWC1, p.369; MWC2, pp.209-213, 220; PW, 202.

Presentation Convent (Mullingar) MWC2, pp.62-63.

Raharney (Killucan) MWC2, pp.289-294.

Rahue/Rahugh or Rathugh (Rahugh) JAPMDI, 3, pp.526-527; MWC1, p.422; Ronan Bagnell, Rahugh, (typescript), (WL).

Rathaspick (Rathaspick) MWC1, pp.441-471.

Rathconnell (Rathconnell) MWC2, pp.221-228.

Rathconrath (Rathconrath) JAPMDI, 2, p.561; 3, p.526; 4, pp.490-493; MWC1, pp.423-426; MWC2, p.351.

Rathduff (Moylisker) JAPMDI, 9, p.557; MWC1, pp.427-428; MWC2, pp.364-378.

Rathgarve (Rathgarve) JAPMDI, 5, p.274.

Mullingar Church and Burial-ground.

'The Protestant Church (St. Mary's) contains a good many modern mural monuments to the families of L'Estrange, Fetherstonhaugh, Swift, Barlow, Tuite, etc.; two of these monuments in the north transept are at such a height that since the removal of the gallery it is impossible to see their inscriptions.

'In the south transept there is a mural monument on which, owing to the lettering not being coloured, the inscription cannot be read without the aid of a ladder; the Sexton, Charles Winters, has kindly supplied me with the following copy of it :—

Under this Monument in a vault is deposited the Body of Hugh Bowen, lineal heir of the House of . . pton in Pembrokeshire, South Wales, who for the space of 44 years held the post of Collector of Trim, during which time he behaved as a pious and good Christian, faithful Subject, and affectionate Husband, tender Father and sincere Friend, and kind Master, beloved and lamented by all acquaintances. Departed 22nd May 1724, Aged 67. By his side is deposited the Body of Anne his wife, Daughter of Wilm Jones of Rathconrath, Esqr, whose truly pious and good life, with her constant Care and Love of her Children, before and after her Husband's decease made her the object of their dutiful regard, admired and beloved by all that knew her. Departed 23rd Decr 1738, Aged 73. Grateful to the memory of such excellent Parents, their Children have erected this Monument.

A memorial inscription from *JAPMD* 9(4) 1915

Rathgraff (Rathgarve) JAPMDI, 4, pp.494-497.

Rathowen (Rathaspick and Russagh) JAPMDI, 12, pp.563-564; MWC1, pp.513-517 and 429-440.

Rathwire (Killucan) MWC2, pp.170-171

Relick (Piercetown) MWC1, pp.278-279; MWC2, pp.379-389.

Reynella (Rathconnell) MWC2, pp.230-224

Russagh (Russagh) MWC1, pp.472-512.

St. Mulchan's (Killulagh) JAPMDI, 2, p.374.

Scarden (Killucan) MWC1, pp.72-74.

South Hill (Castletowndelvin) MWC2, pp.348-349.

Stonehall (Stonehall) JAPMDI, 11, pp.241-245; MWC1, pp.518-527; PW, pp.202-203.

Streete (Street) Riocht Na Midhe, 4 (3), pp.28-29, 1969; MWC, pp.570-610

Taghmon (Taghmon) JAPMDI, 12, pp.126-127; MWC1, pp.631-637.

Teaghbogan/ Taghboyne (Churchtown) JAPMDI, 8. p.181. MWC1, p.638.

Templecross or Tristernagh (Kilbixy) JAPMDI, 5, pp.115-119; 6 pp.609-610; WGP; MWC1, pp.245-253.

Templeoran (Templeoran) MWC1, pp.271-272; MWC2, pp.354-363.

Templepatrick (Templepatrick or Moyvore) MWC1, pp.276-277; Sr. Alberto Savaglia Cormack, Graveyard Inscriptions, Templepatrick, Moyvore (typescript)(WL).

Tubberclare Church (Kilkenny West) MWC2, p.350.

Tyrell's Pass or Tyrellspass (Clonfad/Newtown) JAPMDI, 11, pp.344-345; MWC1, pp 639-640; Matt Poynton and Tom O'Neill, St. Sinan's, Tyrellspass, (typescript), (WL).

Walshestown (Mullingar) Micheál Ó Conláin, Cemetery records for Walshestown, (typescript), (WL).

Wilson's Hospital (Lackan) MWC2, p.277.

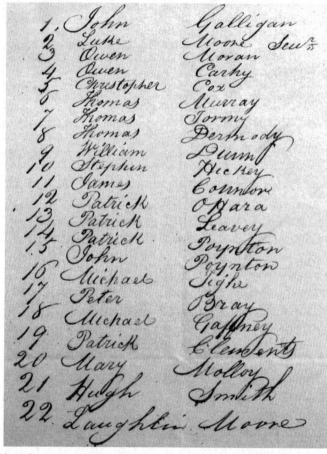

List of persons tried at Mullingar Assizes for Illicit Distillation
'i.e for making whiskey or Poitín' - see page 44.

Chapter 12   Education

A state-supported national school system was introduced in Ireland in 1831. For much of the previous century, until the Catholic Relief Act of 1782, Catholics had been banned from teaching or running schools but many children were taught in 'Hedge Schools', ie any place of shelter that could be found. A. Coogan, *The Diocese of Meath ancient and modern*, 3 vols. Dublin, 1862, 1864 and 1870 gives an account of early Westmeath schools. It may be useful to note that a 'National School' is a state school for ages up to approx. 12; and a 'Secondary School is for ages 12- 18. The Second Report of the Commissioners of National Education, 1835 specified that a register be kept, recording the daily attendance of scholars. Where these registers survive they can be a very valuable source of information. Details recorded include: date of entrance; pupil's name and age; religious denomination, address, occupation or means of living of parents, name and county of the last National School which the pupil attended. There were generally separate registers kept for boys and girls. As in other counties, small rural schools have been amalgamated with larger schools and the registers generally transferred with them.

Records of the Commissioners for National Education in Ireland 1832 – 1924 are held at the NAI. A card index arranged by county may be consulted in the Reading Room. These records are mainly of interest to those whose ancestors worked in the primary school system. Further information on NAI education records may be viewed at www. nationalarchives.ie A list of all National (Primary) schools and second level schools may be viewed at www.departmentofeducation.ie and also at www.schooldays.ie/primary-schools-in-ireland/primary-Westmeath also www.schooldays.ie/secondary-schools-in-ireland/Westmeath

The following is a list of some Westmeath national schools which hold records prior to 1930 showing name of school, parish where the school is situated, date of earliest register and location of the record. The location is usually in the particular school.

Key to the following table:

B	Boys	GI	Girls Infants
BI	Boys Infants	M	Mixed
G	Girls		

Name of School	Parish	Earliest Date	Location of Registers
Athlone, St. Mary's	St. Mary's, Athlone	1878	School
Athlone, St. Peter's	SS. Peter & Paul, Athlone	1902	School
Ballinea	Mullingar	c.1900	See Kilpatrick
Ballinagore	Castletown-Geoghegan	1891	School
Ballynacarrigy	Balynacarrigy/Sonna	1914	School
Ballycomoyle	Castlepollard	1863	Castlepollard School
Balrath	Castlepollard	1925	See Castletown, Finea
Baylin, St. Ciaran's	Moate	B.1924 G.1926	School
Blackberry Lane, Athlone	St. Mary's Athlone	1870	See Cornamaddy
Boher	Ballymore	B.1900 G.1902	School
Carpenterstown	St. Feichin's Fore	1863	See Fore

Castlepollard Parochial	Rathgraffe	1872	School
Castlepollard St. Michaels	Castlepollard	1876	Locally. School from approx. 1914
Castletown, Finea, St. Michaels	Castlepollard	1948	School (see Balrath & Tullystown)
Castletown-Geoghegan, St. Michael's	Castletown-Geoghegan	1938 B.1904 G.1904	School
Clonmellon	Clonmellon/Killallon	1913	School
Cloran (Meath)	Clonmellon/Killallon	1917	See Clonmellon
Collinstown, St. Mary's	St. Mary's, Collinstown	1905	School
Coosan	St. Mary's Athlone	1865	School
Coralstown	Kinnegad	1924	School
Cornamaddy	St. Mary's Athlone	1885	School
Crowenstown, St. Patrick's	Delvin	1881 1951	School
Curraghmore	Mullingar	1884	School

Dalystown	Rochfortbridge	1902	School
Dean Kelly	St. Peters & Paul, Athlone	1918	School
Downs	Kinnegad	G.1872 B.1892	School
Drumraney	Drumraney	G.1886 B.1916 M.1880	School
Dysart	Dysart	B.8.1872 G.5.1872	
Edmonton, St. Patrick's	Killucan	1925	School
Empor, Scoil Naomh Bhride,	Miltown	B.1906 G.1924	School
Finea, St. Mary's	Castlepollard	1910	School
Fore, St. Feichin's	St. Feichin's Fore	1869-	School
Gainstown	Mullingar	B.1869 G.1869	School
Gehanstown/Archerstown	Clonmellon/Killallon	1867	See Clonmellon

Statistics.]—In 1824, according to Protestant returns, the number of schools in *Westmeath* was 216, of scholars 9,919, of male scholars 5,740, of female scholars 3,820, of scholars whose sex was not specified 359, of scholars connected with the Established Church 1,533, of scholars connected with Presbyterian communities 5, of scholars connected with other communities of Protestant dissenters 1; of scholars connected with the Roman Catholic community 8,249, of scholars whose religious connection was not ascertained 131; and, according to Roman Catholic returns, the number of schools was 216, of scholars 10,097, of male scholars, 5,994, of female scholars 4,057, of scholars whose sex was not specified 46, of scholars connected with the Established Church 1,556, of scholars connected with Presbyterian communities 5, of scholars connected with other communities of Protestant dissenters 36, of scholars connected with the Roman Catholic community 8,350, of scholars whose religious connection was not ascertained 150. The statistics of educational and ecclesiastical matters for 1834, are returned according to the diocesan divisions; and may be estimated for Westmeath by reference to the article MEATH (DIOCESE OF): which see. At the close of 1843, the National Board had in full operation within the county 44 schools, conducted by 30 male and 22 female teachers, attended by 2,981 male and 2,591 female scholars, and aided, during the year, with £526 8s. 4d. in salaries, £35 8s. in free stock, and £76 12s. 5d. in school-requisites at half-price.

Statistics relating to Education in Westmeath
from the *Parliamentary Gazetteer of Ireland Vol.III (1846)*

Glascorn	Mullingar	c.1900	See Kilpatrick
Inchmore Island	Tubberclair	1905	National Archives
Irishtown	Milltown	1872	See Milltown Rathconrath
Johnstown	Delvin	1884	St. Tola's, Killough, Delvin
Kilbeggan, Scoil an Chlochair	Kilbeggan	1919	School
Killallon (Meath)	Clonmellon/Killallon	1867	Clonmellon
Killough	Delvin	1880	St. Tola's, Killough, Delvin
Kilpatrick	Mullingar	1980	School
Kinnegad, St. Etchen's	Kinnegad	1985 B 1901 G 1913	School
Knockaville	Killucan	1872	Westmeath County Library CD(restricted access)
Lacken and Laney	Multyfarnham	1895	See Multyfarnham
Loughanavally St. Baoithin's	Dysart	1873	School

Milltownpass, St. Joseph's	Rochfortbridge	1915	School
Moate, Convent Primary School	Moate	1904	School
Moate, St. Oliver Plunkett Boys	Ardagh /Clonmacnoise	1872	School
Mount Temple, An Ghrianan	Moate	1919	School
Moyvore	Milltown	B.1907 G.1914	School
Mullingar, St. Colman's	Mullingar	1979	School
Newbristy	Milltown	1870	Milltown, Rathconrath
Presentation Junior School	Mullingar	1883	School
Raharney, St. Mary's	Killucan	1895	School
Rahugh, Scoil Aodha Naofa	Kilbeggan	1901	School
Rathowen (2) St. Thomas (Cof I)	Rathaspic	1894	School
Rathwire, St. Joseph's	Killucan	1921	School
Rochfortbridge, Convent Primary School	Rochfortbridge	G.1893 B.1896	School

Rochfortbridge, Scoil Bhride	Rochfortbridge	1906	School
Rosemount /Kilcumreragh		B.1873 G.1894	School
Rosmead	Clonmellon/Killallon	1872	See Clonmellon
Sonna	Ballynacarrigy	1939 B.1873	School
Streamstown	Clara (Horseleap)	B.1920 G.1930	School
Tang	Drumraney/Tang	1936	School
Taughmon (Carley)	Taughmon	B.1947 G.1910	School
Tubberclare	Tubberclare/Glasson	B.1923 G.1897	School
Tullystown	Castlepollard	1919	Castletown, Finea
Walshestown	Mullingar	c.1900	See Mullingar
Whitehall, Scoil Dhiarmada	Coole (Mayne)	1873	School

The following secondary schools date from the late 1800s and early 1900s:

St. Finian's College Mullingar built under the auspices of Bishop Gaffney as a diocesan seminary was first occupied in 1908 and continues to operate as a second level institute. From 1802 to 1908 the diocesan seminary was based in Navan, Co. Meath. Full records survive from the 1870s and some before that. Information may be obtained by contacting Fr. Paul Connell, President, St. Finian's College, Mullingar at frpaulconnell@eircom.net

St. Mary's College Mullingar referred to also as 'The Latin' or 'The Heavey Institute' was built in 1856 at the bequest of James Heavey a brewer in the town. Operated until recent times by the Irish Christian Brothers the much modernised school continues to flourish. Some records survive and information on them may be obtained by contacting Mr. Joe O'Meara, Principal at cbsadmin@eircom.net

Wilson's Hospital School Multyfarnham, Co. Westmeath was established at the bequest of Andrew Wilson and opened in 1761. Records for pupils from April 1761 are held at the school. Information on these records may be obtained by contacting the school at wilsonsh@whs.ie

Marist Brothers Athlone. The Marist Brothers arrived in Athlone in 1884 and quickly became involved in the education of boys. The Marist College still flourishes today and information on surviving records may be obtained by contacting the principal at tbmarist@gmail.com

Belvedere Orphan Institution, or the Belvedere Charity 1842 – 1943 was established in Tyrrellspass, and provided care for orphaned girls who were to be brought up in the Protestant faith. Managed by a board of trustees its funds were organised and distributed through the Offices of the Commissioners of Charitable Donations and Bequests, Clare Street, Dublin. (Daniel Dunne, The Belvedere Orphan Institution 1842-1943, unpub. thesis, NUI Maynooth, 1997). Requests for information from the records may be addressed to the Offices of the Commissioners at Clare Street, Dublin. Names of children in the orphanage are recorded in the 1901 and 1911 census www.nationalarchives.ie. The children also participated in the folklore survey 1937-39 under Tyrrellspass No. 2 School.

Franciscan Friary Multyfarnham provided secondary school educational facilities between 1899 and 1954. While records do not survive *The Franciscan College Annual* which commenced in 1932 contains many interesting articles and photographs relating to its early years. The annuals are available to researchers at the Franciscan Library, Dun Mhuire, Seafield Road, Killiney, Co. Dublin.

JOLLY, JOHN SWIFT (1876 – 1943) Surgeon

Dr Jolly was born in Athlone and qualified as a medical doctor in Trinity College, Dublin. He emigrated to England and became surgeon in St Peter's Hospital in London. He achieved an international reputation as a urologist and contributed much on the subject in medical journals. His patients included Lloyd George, Lord Birkenhead, the Duke of Alba and the Maharaja of Bilkaneer.

KAVANAGH, THOMAS (1820 – 1882) Soldier

Born in Mullingar he joined the Indian Civil Service, where he spent many years. At the outbreak of the Indian Mutiny in 1857, he escaped, disguised as a native. Later, he re-entered the occupied area and guided a relief column through the back streets of a city. This feat was described in a citation as "one of the most daring ever attempted" and won for him the Victoria Cross.

Extract from *Worthies of Westmeath*
by Jeremiah Sheehan, Wellbrook Press 1987.

136

Chapter 13   Family Names and Histories

Information on many individual families has been generated by family members or historians and many family histories exist (published and unpublished) but they usually deal with prominent families. They can be difficult to find, as many were printed in small numbers and distributed within families. Some can be accessed through Google Books or similar programmes which make facsimiles available on the internet. Family histories and pedigrees are also published in periodicals A list of such titles is included here, and others are listed in e.g. *Sources for Irish Family History*, Flyleaf Press (Dublin 2001).

The principal Irish families in Westmeath in the twelfth century were MacGeoghegan; O'Mulbrenan or Brenan, O'Coffy, O'Mullady, O'Malone, O'Daly, O'Higgins, Magawly, Magan, O'Shannagh, (afterwards changed to Fox), O'Finilan and O'Cuishin. After the settlement of the Anglo Normans in Leinster in 1172 Norman families arrived including Lacy, Petit, Tuite, Hussey, D'Alton, Delamare, Dillon, Nugent, Hope, Ware, Nangle, Ledewich, Geneville, Dardis, Gaynor, and Constantine. The families of Darcy, Johnes, Tyrrell, Fitzgerald, Owen, and Piers also settled over the next few centuries. After the 1641 Rebellion, further English families obtained grants of confiscated lands, includimg Pakenham, Wood, Cooke, Stoyte, Reynell, Winter, Levinge, Wilson, Judge, Rochfort, Handcock, Bonynge, Gay, Handy, Ogle, Middleton, Swift, Burtle, and St. George. Other families of note who either purchased or inherited land were those of Smith, Fetherston, Chapman, O'Reilly, Purdon, Nagle, Blaquiere and North.

Many books have been published covering Irish surnames, including:
Robert E. Matheson, *Special Report on Surnames in Ireland,* Dublin 1909
Robert E. Matheson, *Varieties and synonyms of surnames and Christian names in Ireland,* Dublin, 1901. Sir Robert E. Matheson was Registrar-General for Ireland.
Edward MacLysaght, *More Irish families and Supplement to Irish families,*Galway, 1960, *A Guide to Irish surnames,* Dublin, 1964, *Irish families; their names, arms and origins,* Dublin, 1972 and *Surnames of Ireland,* Blackrock, 1985.

Surname Distribution in Griffith's Primary Valuation

To indicate the distribution of surnames in County Westmeath, a table showing the most common surnames was compiled from the surname indexes of Griffith's Valuations Survey (1854). The table below, lists the 20 most numerous surnames and indicates the barony in which they were most common at the time. - see map on page 139.

	Surname	Total Number	Barony with most occurrences (no.)
1	Kelly	282	Moycashel (47)
2	Cormack/ McCormack	243	Fore (31)
3	Fagan	239	Fore (141)
4	Daly	213	Moycashel (66)
5	Reilly	206	Fore (53)
6	Smith/ Smyth	189	Fore (55)
7	Farrell	163	Kilkenny West (32)
8	Lynch	123	Fore (36)
9	Moran	121	Kilkenny West (39)
10	Duffy	111	Moycashel (24)
11	Keegan	103	Moycashel (21) Kilkenny West (21)
12	Murphy	99	Fore (21)
13	Connor/ Connors	96	Moyashel and Magheradernon (20)
14	Murtagh	94	Fore (28)
15	Clarke	92	Fore (14) Rathconrath (14)
16	Byrne	90	Clonlonan (13) Moyashel and Magheradernon (13)
17	Brennan	88	Moycashel (43)
18	Walsh	87	Moyashel and Magheradernon (19)
19	Kenny	86	Moygoish (18)
20	Coffey	84	Moycashel (15)

1 *Fore (part in Meath)*
2 *Moygoish*
3 *Corkaree*
4 *Delvin*
5 *Kilkenny West*
6 *Rathconrath*
7 *Moyashel and Maheradermon*
8 *Farbill*
9 *Brawny*
10 *Clonlonan*
11 *Moycashel*
12 *Fartullagh*

Cormack/McCormack
Fagan
Reilly
Smith/Smyth
Lynch
Murphy
Murtagh
Clarke

Kenny

Farrell
Keegan
Moran

Connor/Connors
Walsh

Byrne

Brennan
Coffey
Kelly
Daly
Duffy
Keegan

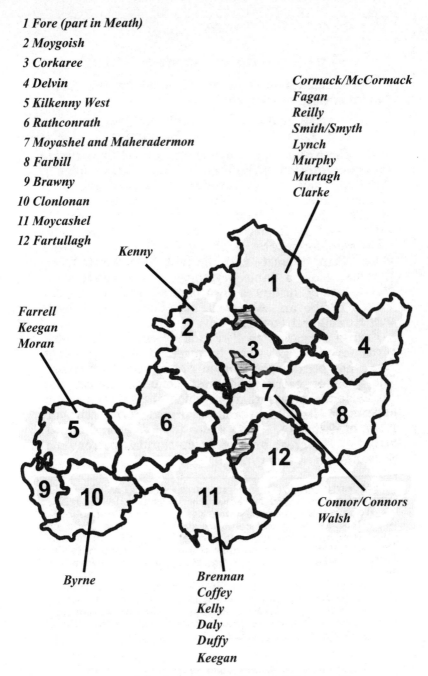

A map of the baronies in County Westmeath
including the 20 most numerous surnames which occur in
Griffith's Primary Valuation. - see opposite page.

17

§ 2—Surnames of the Sean-Gaill

The surnames brought into Ireland by the Anglo-Normans were of four kinds :—

1. Patronymic.   3. Occupative.
2. Local.   4. Descriptive.

1. The Norman patronymic was formed by prefixing Fitz (a corruption of the French " fils," Latin " filius"), denoting " son of," as Fitz-Gerald, Fitz-Gibbon, Fitz-Herbert, Fitz-Simon. The English added " -son," as Richardson, Williamson ; or merely the genitive suffix " -s," as Richards, Williams. Welsh patronymics were formed by prefixing " ap" or " ab," from older " Map," cognate with the Irish Ṁᴀc, which, when it came before a name beginning with a vowel or h, was in many instances incorporated with it, as Ab Evan, now Bevan ; Ab Owen, now Bowen ; Ap Howel, now Howell and Powell.

English surnames in " -s" and " -son," and Welsh surnames in " Ap" were, however, at first extremely rare ; they became common only at a much later date.* The type of patronymic most common among the Anglo-Normans was that in which the father's name appears in its simple and unaltered form, without prefix or desinence. Fitz seems to have been dropped early.† The great bulk of Anglo-Norman patronymic surnames are of this type.

---

*The early Anglo-Norman invaders, coming as they did from Wales, were called Ḃ ṙeaċnaiġ, or Welshmen, by the Irish ; but Welshmen they certainly were not, at least to any appreciable extent, as the almost complete absence of Welsh Christian names from among them amply proves. English surnames in " s " and " son " were peculiar to the Danish districts in the North of England, from which few, if any, of the early invaders came.

† Nothing is more common at the present day in certain parts of the country than to hear a man designated. no matter what his surname, as Maurice William or John James, meaning Maurice, son of William, or John, son of James. This is but a survival of the Norman practice.

A page from *Irish Names and Surnames* (Dublin 1923)
by Rev. Patrick Woulfe
which explains the meanings and origins of
Irish first names and surnames

Some published and unpublished titles dealing with Westmeath family names are listed below. Genealogies of all of the major land-holding families are in The Grand Juries of the County of Westmeath from the year 1727 to the year 1853. Ledestown: John Charles Lyons, 1853.

Branigan: See Canton; Nugent; Keane

Canton: Flynn, Michael P., Genealogy of descendants of Canton family Mullingar and Branigan family Killucan/Rathwire since the middle 19th century, with baptisms and marriages of Cantons from Mullingar Parish Registers since the middle eighteenth century, Mullingar, 1994. WL.

Casey: See Kearney

Coffey: Cuffez, A. (André), Coffey Genealogy 2, addendum, Ostende (Belgium), 1986. NLI, GO 314; typescript, WL; Addendum 2, Ostende (Belgium), 1990. NLI GO 603.

Coleman: Daly, Leo, Editor, Life of Coleman of Lynn/Betha Colmán Lainne, translated by Kuno Meyer, Dublin, 1999.

ConlyGeoghegan: Major Conly Geoghegan (of Westmeath) in 'King James' IAL' (Notes on family members pre-1745)

Dalton: Capt. Miles Dalton (of Dundonnell, Westmeath) in 'King James' IAL' (Notes on family pre-1793).

Daly: Cox, Liam, Daly of Kilcleagh (i.e. Castle Daly, Co. Westmeath), 1984. [manuscript]. WL.

DARCY. (No. 2.)

Arms : Same as "D'Arcy," No. 1.

1. SIR WILLIAM "DARCY" of Platten, of Ferbil.

2. John, of Clondaly, co. Westmeath : second son of Sir William ; m. Margaret, dau. of . . . Fitzgerald.

3. Richard, of Clondaly : son and heir of John ; had a brother Nicholas.

4. Edmond, of Clondaly : son of Richard ; d. at Clondaly on 4th March, 1636, aged about 95 years, and b. in Killucan. This Edmond was five times married : first, to Eleanor, daughter of Sir Thomas Nugent of Carlingtown, co. Westmeath, *s. p.;* secondly to Amy, dau. of Ral. Fitzgerald of Timocho ; thirdly, to Mary, dau. of Patrick Cusack of Janestown, co. Westmeath, *s.p.* fourthly, to Kathleen, dau. of Meyler Petit of Ballytrasny, *s.p.;* and fifthly, to Margery, dau. of Richard Nangle of Ballycorky.

5. Richard : son and heir of Edmond ; m. Mary, dau. of James Nugent of Colamb., Wigton ; had three brothers and three sisters : The brothers were—1. Arthur, m. to Margery, dau. of . . . Tankard, of Carbery, county Westmeath ; 2. Christopher, m. to Honora, dau. of Art McTwohill (Art McToole), co. Wicklow ; 3. George, m. to Kathleen, dau. of . . . Wogan, son of Z . . . Wogan of Rathcoffey, co. Kildare ; the sisters were : 1. Margery, m. to Gerard Nangle of Glann, county Longford ; 2. Elis ; and 3. Margaret, who died *s.p.*

6. Edmond Darcy : Richard's son and heir.

'Darcy' from John O'Hart's *Irish Pedigrees.*

Delamere: Memoir of the family of Delamere, Delamar, De La Mer, etc.: of Donore, Streate and Ballynefid. Dublin: R.D. Webb, 1857 (GO Ms. No. 518; LDS Mf. 257821).

Devenish: Sylvester Devenish (Athlone and Roscommon) in 'King James' IAL' (Notes on family members pre 1700).

Dillon: Col. Henry Dillon (of Westmeath) in 'King James' IAL' (Notes on family members pre-1794).

Evans: The last 6 generation of the family of Evans, now represented by Nicholas Evans of Lough Park, Castlepollard, Co. Westmeath. W. Sloane Evans, 1864.

Geoghegan: Craobh de shliocht Chonaill: Geoghegans of Dublin and Westmeath. Joe MacEochagáin. Pub: Galway Pr.pr. 2005. NLI 9B 2603

Gilligan: See Rourke

Grace: Sheffield, Memoirs of the family of Grace, London, 1823.

Halliday: Pedigree of Quaker family of Halliday (Armagh, Westmeath, Dublin et al). Thos. H. Webb. Ms at Friends Hist. Lib.

Hatfield: Papers (e.g. deeds, leases, and pedigrees) relating to; Hatfield of Killimor ..et al. RIA: Upton Papers), and LDS Mf. 101011.

Hanlys: O'Brien, Gearoid and Angela, The Hanlys, O'Hanlys and Hanleys from Kinel-Dofa to Athlone, Athlone, 1991. WL.

Hynes: See King

Keane: Flynn, Michael P., Genealogy of some descendants of Patrick and Margaret Keane, Rathcolman, Mullingar from c.1800. no date. NLI 9292 f28, WL.

Keane: See Macken

Kearney: Flynn, Michael P. Genealogy of descendants of William Kearney and Mary Mulrain, Williamstown, Cornamaddy, Athlone incorporating some info on the Casey family. 1994/1997. NLI, 9292 f29: WL.

King: Doyle, James, A Short History of the family of Henry King and Ann Hynes of Mount Airy Croton-on-Hudson New York, Asheville, NC 28804, 1998. WL.

Levinge: Sir Richard G.A., Jottings for early history of the Levinge family, Dublin, 1873. NLI, WL.; Jottings of The Levinge Family, Dublin, 1877. NLI, WL.; Tracy, Frank, A Short account of the Levinge family and Knockdrin Castle, Co. Westmeath, 2003. [typescript] WL

Lister: Lyster, Henry Lyttelton, Memorials of an ancient house, A History of the family of Lister or Lyster, Edinburgh, 1913. WL.

Locke: The Locke Family and the Distilling Industry in Kilbeggan History Ireland. 1 (2) Summer, 1993, pp 46-50

McGawley: Capt. Patrick McGawley (of Tulliwood, Co. Westmeath) in 'King James' IAL' (Notes on family members pre-1709).

THE MAGANS OF UMMA, PARISH OF BALLYMORE, CO. WESTMEATH

by Liam Cox

This account of the Magans of Umma (now usually rendered Emo) is based on an Ms. found among the papers of the late Dr J. F. Keenan of Ballinalee, Co. Longford, now in the County Library, Mullingar. Dr Keenan made his copy in June, 1931, from an Ms. in the writing of Mr Henry Upton of Coolatore, Moate, which he had "copied from an Ms. he procured somewhere." The account is in Keenan's Book C, pages 11-24. Umma, otherwise Emo, is approximately halfway between the towns of Moate and Ballymore, and was the oldest of the Magan seats.

HUMPHREY MAGAN of Umma, parish of Ballymore, Co. Westmeath, m. Ann. dau. of Sir Richard Owen of Anglesey, North Wales, and had issue,
I.   Richard, of whom presently.
II. Morgan, of Cloney (see Betham Pedigree in Ulster Office and the will of his son Thomas which calls Richard Magan the younger, his cousin), left issue,
    1. Thomas, of Togherstown, High Sheriff in 1706, an active partizan of William III, one of the Commissioners for raising money by Poll Tax, made large purchases of the Forfeited Estates; m. Sarah Morgan and d.s.p. 1710.
    2. Morgan, of Ballysallagh and Togherstown who in 1710 read his recantation and took the Oath of Supremacy, d. 1738 (will dat. 8 Jan 1737, proved 3 Aug. 1738), leaving by his wife Elizabeth, 6 daus. (only 5 known by

From the *Irish Ancestor* Vol.13 (1) 1981, pp.12-15, - see also below

MacGeoghegans: see Mageoghegans.
McKeoghs: McKeoghs of Moyfinn. J. Old Athlone Soc. 1 (4) (1974/75): pp 234-37; 2 (5) (1978); pp. 56-70.
Macken: Flynn, Michael P., Genealogy of descendants of John Macken and Bridget Keane Modranstown, Rathconrath, Cloncullen, Ballymore and Mullingar town since circa 1800, Mullingar, 1994/1995. WL.
Magan: William, Umma-More. The Story of an Irish Family. History of the Magan family of Umma, near Ballymore, Co. Westmeath, from c. 1590. Salisbury; Element Books, 1983; Papers (e.g., deeds, leases, and pedigrees) relating to Magan of Emoe et al. RIA (Upton Papers), and (LDS Mf. 101011).
Magawly: Magawlys of Calry, J. Old Athlone Soc. 1 (2) (1970/71) pp. 61-73; 1 (3) (1972/73) pp. 147-60; 1 (4) (1974/5) pp. 265-6
Mageoghegans: Cox, Liam, The Mageoghegans, A Lecture by Liam Cox, N.T. to Kilbeggan Hist. and Arch. Soc. 10th January, 1969 (typescript). WL; Walsh, Rev. Paul, The Mageoghegans, a lecture by Rev. Paul Walsh at Castletown-Geoghegan 6th December, 1938, Mullingar, 1938. (typescript) WL.
Malone: Malones of Westmeath, Gaelic Gleanings 1 (1) (1981) pp. 9-12; 1 (2) pp. 46-48; 1 (3) pp. 81-84; 1 (4) pp. 127-30; 2 (1) (1982) pp. 9-10

Meares: Meares, Robert, Pedigree of family of Mears long seated in the County of Westmeath sprung from the ancient name of Delamere, Dublin, 1901. NLI Ir9292 m38. WL.

Mongan: Mongan, Norman, A Century of silence: echoes from a Massachusetts landscape; my quest to find my ill-fated granduncle in America, Dublin, 2009.

Mongan, Norman, Toherstown House; Report – archival research on the history of the property and its owners, 1695-2002, unpublished, 2002. WL.

Mulrain: See Kearney

Nangle: Capts. Walter and Geo. Nangle (of Westmeath) in 'King James' IAL' (Notes on family pre – 1700)

Nugent: Flynn, Michael P., Genealogy of descendants of Nugent family Barrtogher, Rathowen and Churchtown (Milltown), Ballinea, Mullingar since the early nineteenth century, Mullingar, [1995]. NLI 1B 1187, WL; Nugent, Claud, Memoir of Robert, Earl Nugent with letters, poems and appendices, London, 1898. NLI, WL; Nugent, Colonel Thomas Nugent, Earl of Westmeath, in 'King James' IAL' (Notes on family members pre 1779).

O'Flaherty: Lt. Col. Morrogh O'Flaherty (of Culvin, Co. Westmeath) in 'King James' IAL' (Notes on family members pre-1768).

O'Hanleys: See Hanlys

Pakenham: O'Donnell, Hugh, Pakenham family of Tullynally Castle, Maynooth, 1967. WL.

Pollard: Coleman, Marie, The History of the Pollard Family of Castlepollard, no date. [typescript] WL.

Robinson: Robinson of Killogeenaghan; a Westmeath Quaker Family. Ir.Anc. 14 (1) (1982) pp. 1-5.

Rochfort: Rochfort, James, The Rochforts, [Kildare], 2000.

Rotheram: Rotheram, Patrick, Rotherams of Crossdrum, Bath, 1991, NLI GO 175. WL.

Rourke: Simmons, Ken, 1851 to 2001; celebrating 150 years in Australia of Francis Rourke and Catherine Gilligan and their family, a history of the ancestry and descendants, Randwick, 2000. WL.

Smyth Papers. [Drumcree, Co. Westmeath]. Anal. Hib. (20) pp. 279-301.

Tyrell: Kelly, Jennifer A., Richard Tyrrell; Elizabethan Captain, Tyrellspass, 1997; Tyrrell, Joseph Henry, A Genealogical history of the Tyrrells, London, 1980. First published privately, 1904.

Chapter 14   Further Reading

There are many published local and organisation histories and also titles that provide background reading on family and local history. This chapter presents titles under three headings namely; background reading and general references on family history, local histories and Irish history. Titles in typescript format may only be available at WL, however an internet search can yield useful results.

Background reading and general references on Family History

See McLysaght references on page 137.

Burke, Bernard and Burke, Ashworth P., *A Genealogical and Heraldic History of the Peerage and Baronetage etc,* London, 1911 (and many other editions) *Burke's Irish Family Records,* London, 1976.

D'Alton, John, Illustrations, *historical and genealogical, of King James' Irish Army List (1689),* 2 vols., 2nd edition, Dublin, [1860].

Ryan, James. *Sources for Irish Family History.* Flyleaf Press, 2001.

The Irish Genealogist, Volumes 1-8 1937-1973, Eneclann, 2005 *(CD-ROM).*

Local Histories

Abbott, Vincent, *A Place called Rahugh,* [Kilbeggan], 1986. NLI 5A 4296, WL; *A Place called Kilbeggan,* Kilbeggan, *c.*1980s. WL

Andrews, J.H., *Mullingar, Historic Towns Atlas, No. 5, Dublin, 1992.*

Bannon, Dermot, *Parish of Mullingar: year of the great jubilee: Pilgrimage to Portloman Sunday, May 21st, 2000 AD,* Mullingar, 2000.

Bond, Georgiana Sidney Macgeough (neé Bond), Family Patchwork, NLI Ms. 18,450, [typescript] WL

Burke, John, *Athlone in the Victorian era,* Athlone, 2006.

Cahill, Sean, O'Brien, Gearoid and Casey, Jimmy, *Lough Ree and its Islands,* Athlone, 2006.

Clarke, Bay, Editor, *Tyrellspass Hello,* Tyrellspass, 2000.

Connell, Paul, Cronin, Denis A. and Ó Dálaigh, Editors, *Irish Townlands: studies in local history,* Dublin 1998. (Chapter on Dysert, Co. Westmeath).

Cox, Liam, *Moate County Westmeath; a history of the town and district,* Athlone, 1981. (contains extensive family references); *Placenames of Westmeath; the baronies of Clonlonan and Kilkenny West,* Moate, 1994.

Daly, Leo, *The Parish of Mullingar,* [Mullingar], 1984; *Titles,* Mullingar, 1981.

Dease, Edmund F., *A complete history of the Westmeath hunt, from its foundation...,* Dublin, 1898. Available on line at www.askaboutireland.ie

Duffy, Christy, *Balrath, Bunbrosna and beyond..* Mullingar, n.d.

Dunne, Daniel, The Belvedere Orphan Institute 1842-1943, unpublished thesis, NUI Maynooth, 1997; *Children of the mounds: a history of the Gainstown/Gaybrook area,* Mullingar, 2003.

Dunne, Daniel, Editor, *The Town at the crossroads, Baile na gCros, a history of Castlepollard, Castletown and Finea parish,* [Castlepollard], [2007].

Egan, Frank, *Athlone's golden mile,* Athlone, 1980.

Egan, Oliver, *Tyrellspass; past and present,* Tyrrellspass, 1986.

Fagan, Patrick, *The Diocese of Meath in the Eighteenth Century,* Dublin, 2001.

Fallon, Rosaleen and Michael, Editor, *Clonown: the history, traditions and culture of a South Roscommon community,* Athlone, 1989.

Farrell, Mary, Editor, *Mullingar; essays on the history of a Midlands Town in the 19th Century,* Mullingar, 2002.

Farrell, Noel, *Exploring Family origins in Athlone,* Longford, 2006; *Exploring Family Origins in Mullingar,* Longford, 2005.

Fitzsimons, Hannah, *The Great Delvin,* [Delvin], 1975.

Flynn, K. and McCormack, S., *Westmeath 1798: A Kilbeggan Rebellion,* [1998].

Gavin, Kieran, *Childhood memories of Moate in the mid 1940's,* [Moate], [2008].

Grouden, Breda, *The Contribution of the Clibborn Family to Moate Town and District,* Moate Historical Society, Occasional Paper No. 4 November 1990. NLI Ir 941 p. 108(4).

Hemstead, Frank, Editor, Foy, Geoffrey, *A life in the Flood Plain of the River Shannon, Athlone,* 1994. (Unpublished). WL.

Hughes, Vera, *The Years between Moate, Co. Westmeath 1956-2006,* Moate, 2007.

Ireland, Department of the Environment, Heritage and Local Government, *An Introduction to the Architectural Heritage of County Westmeath,* [Dublin], 2007.

Keaney, Marian, *Westmeath Local Studies; a guide to sources,* Mullingar, 1982.

Kiernan, Kitty, *A Bibliography of the history of the County of Westmeath in printed books,* Mullingar, 1959 (typescript). WL.

Leask, H.G., *Fore County Westmeath,* Dublin, n.d.

McCormack, Stan, *Kilbeggan past and present,* Kilbeggan, 2006. *Moyvoughley and its hinterland,* [Moyvougley], *c.*1999.

Multyfarnham Parish; *Faith, History, Tradition and Celebration, Jubilee 2000,* Multyfarnham, 2000.

Murtagh, Harman, *Athlone; history and settlement to 1800,* Athlone, 2000.

O'Brien, Brendan, *Athlone Workhouse and the Famine,* Athlone, 1995.

O'Brien, Gearoid, Editor, Clonbonny: a centre of learning, Athlone, 1995; *Athlone Miscellany*, Dublin, 2011; *St. Mary's parish, Athlone; a history,* Longford, 1989.

O'Brien, Seamus, Editor, *A Town in Transition:Post Famine Mullingar,* Mullingar, 2007; *Carn, Killare: a forgotten Westmeath famine village,* Mullingar, 2000; *Famine and Community in Mullingar Poor Law Union, 1845-1849: mud huts and fat bullocks,* Dublin, 1999.

Ó Conláin, Micheál, Editor, *The Castlepollard massacre*; *A collection of reports, from various sources on the state of the country during the 1820's... Mullingar, 1981.* NLI 5B 1786 Ir9413 pl; (typescript) WL; *Mullingar and the Railways 1848-1989*, [Mullingar], 1989. NLI Ir 384 p 31 (4) WL; Editor, *The trial of the Castlepollard Policeman.* [Mullingar], 1982. NLI Ir 9413 p 1: (typescript) WL.

Ó Conláin, Micheál, Editor, Conlan, Thomas, *The Sunny side of old Mullingar*, 3 volumes, Mullingar, 1991. (typescript). WL.

O'Farrell, Padraic, *The Book of Mullingar,* Mullingar, 1986.

Ó Gibealláin, P., *Multyfarnham Abbey Monuments and Memories,* Multyfarnham, 1984.

Sheehan, Jeremiah, Editor, *Beneath the Shadow of Uisneach; Ballymore and Boher,* Ballymore, 1996; *Worthies of Westmeath*, Moate 1987; *The Parish of Clonmellon/Killallon,* [Clonmellon], 2001.

Thorne, Kathleen Hegarty, *They put the flag a-flying; the Roscommon Volunteers 1916-1923,* Oregan, 2005. (includes Athlone Brigade – South Westmeath)

Wallace, Peter, *Multyfarnham Parish History*, Multyfarnham, 1987.

Walsh, Rev. Paul, *Ancient Westmeath*, Gigginstown, Mullingar, 1985; *The Placenames of Westmeath*, Dublin, 1957.

Woods, James, *The Annals of Westmeath,* Dublin, 1908. Available on line at www.askaboutireland.ie

Irish History
Glazier, Ira A., Editor, *The Famine immigrants; lists of Irish immigrants arriving at the port of New York 1846-1851,* 7 vols., Baltimore, 1983-1986.

Journals
Journal of the Old Athlone Society, 1969 –
Riocht na Midhe; records of the Meath Archaeological and Historical Society, Drogheda, 1955 –

Chapter 15

Repositories and Useful Addresses

National Repositories

General Register Office
Convent Road,
Roscommon
www.groireland.ie
Tel.: 090 6632900

GRO Research Facility
3rd Floor, Block 7
Irish Life Centre
Lower Abbey Street
Dublin 1
www.groireland.ie
Tel.: 090 6632900

Land Registry
Central Office
Chancery Street
Dublin 7
www.landregistry.ie
Tel: (353 1) 6707500

Military Archives
Cathal Brugha Barracks
Rathmines
Dublin 6
www.military.ie/
Tel.: (353 1) 8046457

National Archives of Ireland
Bishop Street
Dublin 8
www.nationalarchvies.ie
Tel: (353 1) 4072300

National Library of Ireland
Kildare Street,
Dublin 2.
www.nli.ie. and http://sources.nli.ie/
Tel: (353 1) 6030200

Genealogical Office
(NLI manuscript reading room)
2 Kildare Street,
Dublin 2.
www.nli.ie.
Tel: (353 1) 6030200

Public Record Office of Northern Ireland
2 Titanic Boulevard
Belfast
BT3 9HQ
Northern Ireland
www.proni.gov.uk
Tel.: (+44) 028 90 534800

Registry of Deeds
Henrietta Street
Dublin 1
www.landregistry.ie/eng/
Tel.: (353 1) 6707500

**Representative Church
Body Library**
Braemor Park
Churchtown
Dublin 16
www.library.ireland.anglican.org
Tel: (353 1) 4923979

Royal Irish Academy
19 Dawson Street
Dublin 2.
www.ria.ie
Tel: (353 1) 6762570

Valuation Office
Block 2
Irish Life Centre
Lower Abbey Street
Dublin 1
www.valoff.ie
Tel.: (353 1) 8171000

**Westmeath Repositories and
Organisations**

Dun na Sí Heritage Centre
Moate
Co. Westmeath
www.rootsireland.ie
Tel.: 090 6481183 (see page 153)

Delvin Historical Society
Delvin
Co. Westmeath
www.delvinhistory.com

Old Athlone Society
c/o NIB Building,
Northgate Street
Athlone
Email: oldathlone@online.ie

Westmeath County Library
County Buildings
Mount Street
Mullingar
Co. Westmeath
www.westmeathcoco.ie
Tel: 044 9340781

**Westmeath Archaeological
and Historical Society**
Secretary
Leney
Multyfarnham
County Westmeath.
Email: peterwallace2@eircom.net

Societies and Organisations

**Church of Jesus Christ
of Latter Day Saints**
Mormon Family History Centre
The Willows,
Finglas Road,
Dublin 11
https://familysearch.org/
Tel: (353 1) 8309960

**Huguenot Society of
Great Britain and Ireland**
c/o Sunhaven
Dublin Road
Celbridge
Co. Kildare
www.huguenotsociety.org.uk

Irish Huguenot Archive
www.huguenotsinireland.com/

Irish Jewish Museum
3-4 Walworth Street
South Circular Road
Dublin 8
www.jewishireland.org
Tel:(353 1) 4531797

Presbyterian Historical Society
Church House
Fisherwick Place
Belfast BT1 6DW
Northern Ireland
www.presbyterianhistoryireland.com
Tel.: (048) 09322284

Religious Society of Friends
(Quaker community)
Historical Library
Quaker House
Stocking Lane
Dublin 16
www.quakers.ie
Tel.: (01) 4956890

Society of Genealogists
14 Charterhouse Buildings
Goswell Road
London EC1M 7BA
UK
www.sog.org.uk/

Major Websites:
The websites of the above archives are hugely valuable sources. In addition, however there are other websites of value.

1901 and 1911 Census
www.censusnationalarchives.ie
This excellent site is run by the National Archives above and provides free access to the 1901 and 1911 census data.

www.askaboutireland.ie
This is run by the Library Council of Ireland and is largely aimed at schools. However, it provides access to Griffith's Valuation, to many maps, and also downloads of local histories.

www.irishgenealogy.ie
This government site is a portal to some of the other national websites, but also provides a free search facility for church records in parts of Dublin, Kerry, Carlow and Cork. Addition of further records to the site is planned.

www.rootsireland.ie
This site is run by the IFHF which runs a network of local county Heritage or genealogy centres which have indexed local church records.

The site provides central access to the records of these Heritage centres. Existence of a record can be established free on the site, but a fee will be charged for access to the details.

www.findmypast.ie
This site provides subscription-based access to Prison records (1790-1924); the order books of the Petty Sessions (i.e. a local court for minor cases) from 1850-1910; and a range of other sources (directories, military sources etc.).

www.rootsweb.ancestry.com/~irlsli/sligocountyireland.html.
This excellent site has a range of materials donated by volunteers including transcriptions of church and other records and a forum for Sligo researchers.

http://sources.nli.ie/
A database of manuscripts and articles of Irish relevance in the National Library and in many other archives in Ireland and elsewhere. It is worth a search for the area in which you are interested.

www.familysearch.org
This is the site of the Mormon Church, or Church of Jesus Christ of Latter-day Saints whose Salt Lake City headquarters houses the largest library of genealogical information in the world. Mormon churches usually have a family history section and welcome researchers.

The ruins of Fore Abbey
from *The Saturday Magazine,* 14th October 1837

Dún Na Si Heritage Centre

Moate, County Westmeath, Ireland
Phone: 090 64 81183
International +353 90 64 81183
Fax: 090 64 81661
dunnasimoate@eircom. net

Dún na Sí Heritage Centre and Park was established in 1984. It is owned by the Moate Branch of Comhaltas Ceoltoiri Eireann. We are a gathering of people who work together for the purpose of promoting and preserving our Irish Culture and Heritage. In 1989 we embarked on the task of developing a Genealogical database for County Westmeath. The Centre offers an extensive range of services and products to both individual and special interest groups

Genealogical Research Services
- Single Record Search
- Family Search
- Online Search

Visitor Services
- Research Consultations service
- Location Search
- Same Day Research Service

The Centre is part of a national network of designated genealogical Centres in Ireland and is a member of the Irish Family History Foundation. It is a non-profit enterprise partially funded by the Government Department of Social Protection. All monies accrued from its operations are used to maintain the provision of the service

DESIGNATED HERITAGE CENTRE FOR WESTMEATH
MEMBER OF IRISH FAMILY HISTORY FOUNDATION

Index

N
Nangle 137, 144
Newspapers 105
Newtown 20, 69, 78, 124, 126
Newtownfertullagh 78
Newtownlow 124
Noughaval 20, 64, 69, 120, 121, 124
Nugent 12, 137, 141, 144

O
Occupational Sources 5, 111, 116
O'Flaherty 144
O'Hanleys 144
Oldcastle 73
Ordnance Survey 17, 23, 26, 94

P
Pakenham 137, 144
Pallas 64
Parliamentary Gazetteer 25
Passenger Lists 44
Pass of Kilbride 20, 69, 124
Patent Rolls 89
Penal Laws 61
Pensioners 54
Petty Sessions 50, 152
Petty, Sir William 38
Piercetown 20, 69, 121, 125
Plantation 38
Pollard 144
Poll Book 40
Poor Law Union 18, 22, 26
Portloman 20, 69, 124, 145
Portnashangan 20, 69, 78, 124
Prerogative Will 96, 98, 102
Prerogative Wills 96, 97
Primary Valuation 82, 138, 139
Principal Registry 100
Principal Will 96
Probate 73, 96, 98, 100, 102
Protestants 39, 40, 44, 45

Q
Quaker Cemetery 80, 124

R
Raharney 67, 124, 133
Rahue 124
Rahugh 20, 70, 124, 133, 145

Rathaspick 20, 40, 52, 70, 71, 78, 82, 124, 125
Rathconnell 20, 44, 70, 78, 120, 121, 124, 125
Rathconrath 18, 20, 21, 47, 48, 62, 67, 70, 121, 123, 124, 132, 133, 138, 139, 143
Rathduff 124
Rathgarraf 68
Rathgarve 20, 65, 68, 70, 78, 120, 124, 125
Rathgraff 125
Rathgraffe 73, 129
Rathowen 70, 85, 125, 133, 144
Rathreagh 40
Rathwire 67, 125, 133, 141
Rebellion 42, 137, 147
Reddy 57
Register of Trees 42, 43
Registry of Deeds 7, 86, 95, 101, 104, 150
Reilly 137, 138, 139
Relick 125
Rentals 48, 49, 51
Rent Book 42
Reynella 125
Robinson 144
Rochfort 137, 144
Rochfortbridge 6, 63, 64, 65, 69, 130, 133, 134
Rosemount 47, 66, 123, 134
Rosmead 134
Rostalla 64
Rotheram 144
Rourke 142, 144
Royal Irish Constabulary 9, 117
Russagh 20, 52, 70, 71, 83, 125
Russough 42

S
Scarden 125
Seamen 35
Shrule 40
Smith 4, 6, 7, 50, 137, 138, 139, 160
Smith O'Brien, William 50
Smyth 6, 39, 52, 138, 139, 144
Soldiers 102, 103
Sonna 65, 72, 128, 134
South Hill 125

Pakenham Hall
from
A Complete History of The Westmeath Hunt from its Foundation
by Edmund F. Dease (Dublin 1898)

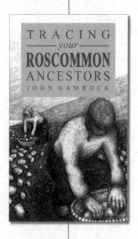

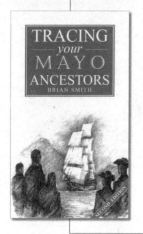

Other Titles From

⟆FLYLEAF PRESS

Tracing Your Cork Ancestors
by Tony McCarthy & Tim Cadogan
ISBN 978-1-907990-01-4

Tracing Your Donegal Ancestors
by Helen Meehan & Godfrey Duffy
ISBN 978-0-9539974-9-7

Tracing Your Dublin Ancestors
by James G. Ryan & Brian Smith
ISBN 978-0-9563624-1-4

Tracing Your Galway Ancestors
by Peadar O'Dowd
ISBN 978-0-9563624-2-1

Tracing Your Limerick Ancestors
by Margaret Franklin
ISBN 0-9539974-4-8

Tracing Your Mayo Ancestors
by Brian Smith
ISBN 978-0-9563624-3-8

Tracing Your Roscommon Ancestors
by John Hamrock
ISBN 978-0-9539974-7-3

Tracing Your Sligo Ancestors
by James G. Ryan
ISBN 978-1-907990-04-5

Irish Church Records
ed. by James G. Ryan
ISBN 0-9539974-1-3

For Full Details Visit
www.flyleaf.ie

Sept 2012